I Had To Go There
To Get Here

I Had To Go There
To Get Here

IT IS WHAT IT IS

Phyllis Ames-Bey

Published in the United States of America

ISBN 978-1-963379-81-5 (SC)

Phyllis Ames-Bey Publishing
222 West 6th Street
Suite 400, San Pedro, CA, 90731
www.stellarliterary.com

Order Information and Rights Permission:

Quantity sales. Special discounts might be available on quantity purchases by corporations, associations, and others. For details, contact the publisher at the address above.

For Book Rights Adaptation and other Rights Permission. Call us at toll-free 1-888-945-8513 or send us an email at admin@stellarliterary.com.

CONTENTS

OPEN LETTER TO MY SON.. 13

MY TESTIMONY 19

SECTION ONE-PETITIONS TO GOD 25

SECTION TWO-SIDE TITLED POEMS 37

SECTION THREE-DECEASED ONES 85

SECTION FOUR-ASSOCIATES... 91

SECTION FIVE-SUICIDAL THOUGHTS 103

SECTION SIX-THE INNER ME-POERTY AND POEMS 123

SECTION SEVEN-COMPANIONS 151

SECTION EIGHT-SONGS: 259

    Inspirational 259

    Ballads 271

    Rap 317

SECTION NINE-PRAYERS TO GOD 327

DEDICATION

Giving honor to God, I truly thank him for the completion of this book. It was his dedicating spirit within me which enabled me to complete it within six days.

I wish to dedicate this book to my son, Saleem El-Amin Ali-Bey for his love and understanding. I also wish to dedicate it to my mother Leona; my sisters Genovia, Estella and Belinda and my grand children and relatives. Last, I wish to dedicate it to Darryl Butcher, who stuck by me and encouraged me daily to do something with my writings.

ACKNOWLEDGMENTS

I thank Reverend Gould, Reverend Lester C. Smith and my church family and friends. I thank my friends at work-namely Maria, Blanca, Lucy, Diana, Ora, Roslyn, Mamie and Mattie.

I also thank my personal friends Connie Johnson, Joan Ginns, Vanessa Chapman, Yvonne Hollinger, Albert Newman, Bob Wellons, Calvin Marshall, Joyce Lowery, Val Singleton.

Finally, thanks go to Garry Core who gave me information on how to write and publish the book and George Butler of Butler Prestige Photography who provided the picture.

INTRODUCTION

I began to type the writings on Thursday, October 12, 2009 at 8:00am and completed the typing Tuesday, October 20, 2009 at 10:00pm.

This book consist of poems, poetry, songs and prayers about life and death experiences. It addresses making choices. The best choice one could make is to live. Live life in the spirit of God, for he will manifest love, favor and any other needs to be provided.

OPEN LETTER TO MY SON

OPEN LETTER TO MY SON

SALEEM,

Thank you. I'm not thanking you for being my son. I am thanking you for being my everything. You were my determination. My true loved one. I am thanking you for the love, affection and understanding during the good times and the bad times. I am thanking you for determining to be a man. Most of all I am thanking you for finding ALLAH.

There will be struggles in your life; but if you talk to him, he'll help you through them. Just talk to him like you talk to anyone. Have him with you always. Thank him for everything.

I am hoping this book will inspire you to get your business, "Silent Brotherhood of America, Inc." off the ground. You can by doing something with the songs you write, doing the spoken word and greeting cards for me or any thing you set your mind to.

Incidentally, don't become angry over the rap song I wrote to young adults on behalf of their moms when you were 15.

I will close my letter to you with the MOORISH AMERICAN PRAYER.

ALLAH the Father of the Universe, the Father of Love, Truth Peace, Freedom and Justice. ALLAH is my Protector, my Guide, and my Salvation by night and by day, through His Holy Prophet, DREW ALI. (Amen).

Love,
Mom

SALEEM

I watched the years as they went by
    Sometimes I felt hopeless, sometimes I cried
I cried because I felt with you
    My time I shared was but a few
I watched the years as they went by
    Hoping *he'd* give to you the love I denied
What I *did* see made me feel good
    Because you grew close like father and son should
I watched the years as they went by
    And now I finally realize
That it was very important to me
    For us to live as a family.

SALEEM

Saleem wants to go to school somewhere down south this year
    He tells me that he cannot learn if he goes to school up here
He stated he has lots of friends keeping him from learning some days
    He wants to do the best he can while he feel like changing his ways

But you see he doesn't fool me, he's learned of my life
    The one in which he had watched me suffering stress and strife
He heard my husband say to me "I love you Phyl me dear
    And if you ever need someone remember that I'm here."

"I still love you this I know." He heard him say to me
    And my response was, "No you don't, why don't you leave me be?
You've been running long before we met and women still call our home
    You gave to them all of your time and left me home alone

Since we're apart-let's talk
For at times-you were good for me
You've deceived my heart
But it's a new day-and it will mend, you'll see."

MY TESTIMONY

MY TESTIMONY

This is my Testimony-and I hope it will lead
You-to the Holy Trinity-for They will set you free.
I met Reverend Lester C. Smith-on my job one day.
He said, "Child why don't you come on,
     Let me teach you to walk God's way."
I said, "Rev.-God don't want me no more-I'm too old now.
   And if He did-why did he allow-me-to go down?"
"I'm drinking, I gambling and I'm even running the streets."
   He said, "Hush child-you're the very person He wants to meet."
"He'll cleanse your heart, your mind, your body and your soul.
   He'll even give you blessings more precious than gold."

Well one Sunday I was on my way to play some cards.
   You know, gamble, dance and drink a little booze.
But God said, "Phyllis, Phyllis, your body is my temple
   and today it will not be abused or misused."
I had to walk pass the church to get to where we played
   And as I tried to walk by, I entered the church, instead.
Service was just about over and Rev. put me on the spot
   when he acknowledged my presence, but he didn't say a lot.
He said, "How old are you child?" I couldn't lie-so I said, "23."
   Though I knew in a few days, 24 was the age I would be.

He said, "My Goodness, I had no idea you were that age.
   I thought you were in your teens-but at any rate
Where were you going and why are you here?"
   I said, "*You* know where I was going, but I felt Jesus near.
I came to be saved and be baptized in Jesus name.
   I want to do his will, but most of all, I want to change."

Reverend Smith prayed for and with me.
     I was redressed in a cap and white robe.
He had his arms wide open waiting
     to welcome me into his fold.
He reminded me of God, with his pure white hair
     and the congregation witnessed my baptism, in the mirror.
And I cried, with hands outstretched towards him
     And these are the word I cry today; I can't print the word to the
hymn.
I *will* say, "Father I stretch my hand to thee, to do with me as thy will
     And please continue to walk with me and let my peace be still."

I'M NOT ASHAME

I was lost-deep in sin-and caught up in the world
 And was ashame—of the shape-I was in
But I fell-to my knees-and cried, "God help-me please."
 For-I was tired-of the places-I had been
I would drink-day and night-when I was of the world.
 I would drink-to the point-where I'd fight.
I was ashame-of the way-I was living—each day
 To the point-where I gave up-on life
I would go-to the bar-when I got off from work
 And I'd smoke-in anyone's car
Someone said, "Child. Wake up-for you're on-the-wrong-path.
 Don't you know-that you're going—too far?"
Well one day-I woke up-and I went to a church
 The first step-that I took-was so tough
Full of shame on my knees-I cried, "God-help me-please
 For the road that I'm traveling is rough."
Then a voice softly said, "Are you ashame to love me,
 and ashame—you don't know-how to pray?
Look deep down in your heart-if you want a new start
 and I promise-I'll show you—the way.
I will always-be there-full of 'Justus' and grace
 In all ways-I will show you-I care.
Are you ashame to love me-serve and praise-and be free?
 Come unto me-for your sins-I—did-bear."
And I cried, "Jesus-I'm not ashame—to love you.
 Lord-not ashame to serve and praise you
 God-I'm not ashame—to lift you up
 for when I called you-I know-that-you-came."

tune available

PETITIONS TO GOD

THE WELFARE OF MY FRIEND

She's a lovely lady she's a pearl
To the man she loves she'd be his world
To all who stand and stare in awe
She'd let them know he is her all.

    To have, hold and love forever more
    'cause faith in love had been restored.
    She was hurt by love and hurt by sin,
    She was hurt by thoughts of letting love in.

Within her heart she knew she must
Find someone soon whom she could trust
She couldn't trust love she couldn't trust men
She couldn't trust anyone to be her friend.

    But one day she fell to her knees
    And began to pray saying, "Dear GOD please
    Send me that one to be a friend
    And let the loneliness come to and end."

"And let him walk beside my side
And when there's a need to him confide
That I want him to be my man
To talk with me and understand."

    "To kiss my lips, my nose, my eyes
    Say I love you when we arise.
    To hold my hands and squeeze me tight
    And rock me gently through the night."

"To lift me up within his arms
To calm me when I feel alarmed
Dear GOD send someone I can trust
Let him share his love that is a must."

"Let him be warm in words and deeds
And be sincere in sharing our needs
But most of all just be my friend
And love me deeply from within."

WHAT AM I TO DO

I know life is not a gamble so why do I take chances
On living as though it's a bet with losses and advances
Why is it I live my life seeking to be gratified
Just what is it that I seek in order to be satisfied.

I used to think that it was love but now some how I've found
I still take my chances even with true love around
I take them when I experience joy and peace of mind
I take them when I experience happiness some of the time.

Just what is it I'm seeking what am I living for
What's causing me to take chances what is it I must endure
More pain, hurt and suffering—is that truly what I desire
Probably cause of me feeling I don't deserve to be satisfied.

"God please give me the answer to what I'm searching for
Help me to live as you see fit for now and evermore.
Take me into your loving arms, hear my silent plea
Tell me what I am to do and what you want of me."

TOLD OF STATUS TOO LATE

Too late I found that I was drawn—to married men, and that was wrong.
A.D. I had known less than a month—was matter of fact and very blunt.
You see, with him I had to say—that I looked forward to each day.
Because I didn't know—if here I'd be, but I did know I could be me.

LaNair, I had known over a year-and every so often I'd wipe a tear
Because-he is-my ideal man, but I'll find one single-if I can.
I have known Champ, since 69, he assured me everything would be fine.
Why couldn't I have all three rolled into one-to share my night when day is
done?

I want the feelings I possess-from a single man for true happiness.
Then I can be myself for sure-for my problem is I must mature
Into being the woman I wish to be-and if I try-I will succeed.
But for some reason-I feel I can't, because I'm afraid to take the chance.

For I've loved hard-and I've loved long, and I'm tired of feeling weak-I
    must be strong.
I am no one's type-and this I know, and in feeling empty-I'm on the go.
"Dear God, help me, I want to live and I have plenty of love to give.
It's just that I can't stand the pain-and don't want to experience it again.

So I play cold, cruel, knowing and tough-cause I have had about enough.
All I ask is that one man be-honest, patient and loving in dealing with me.
Please send that special one my way-please answer my prayer this very day,
For I am tired of married men-and I want them only as a friend."

FOR ONCE IN MY LIFE

For once in my life I'd like to succeed
That is my desire and that is my need
For once in my life I want a home
Full of warmth and love instead of being alone

    For once in my life I want to feel loved
    I want to be squeezed, kissed and hugged
    For once in my life I want a sweet caress
    Not hide my feelings and suffer duress.

For once in my life I want to be me
Alive and vibrant and feeling happy
For once in my life I want to live
I want to receive as well as give.

    For once in my life I want a man to myself
    Not someone to share with everyone else
    For once in my life—my dear God please
    Listen to my desires and let them be.

MY GOAL

I choose life and good
    Over death and evil
        And I'll love GOD
            With my whole heart.

I'll walk in his ways
    Keep his commandments
        For he gave me
            A brand new start.

I'll keep his judgments
    And his statues
        And I will
            Definitely walk in love.

There's no other way
    I'd conduct myself
        For I'm blessed
            By GOD above.

THE RESULTS

A veil was lifted from my eyes
　　This I realize
A veil was lifted from my heart
　　And that was when I cried
To GOD above to help me
　　Make my burdens light
Clean my heart and clean my mind
　　Make everything alright.

I can feel a calmness
　　While going about my days
I can feel additional strength
　　While going about my way
To being the child I requested to be
　　When I prayed on my knees
For him to help me to be strong
　　And stop me from doing wrong.

LOO K UP AND LIVE

I have searched to know
　　Exactly why do I exist
What is it God want me to do
　　While death is what I resist
Is *that* what I'm suppose to do
　　Have I been here before
Was I too weak-minded the last time
　　Am I back to try once more
To look up and live my life
　　To the fullest as God meant
Ministering unto others
　　Instead of feeling so hell-bent
To escape all this misery
　　E scape the loneliness
I must be here to do God's will
　　If so, then I am blessed.

THE CHOICE

From here on
    I will observe
        N o holidays, no seasons
            No special hours
                Or times
                    For any reasons
It causes me feelings of pain and stress
And causes me to feel very depressed

I'll live each day I awake-anew
And as my last with what I do

I'll live in God-walk in his steps
Learn of him more and avoid the depths.

I am a new person
Living for and in God
And in his word
I will abide.

POEM OR SONG FOR MAMIE'S CHURCH

There are times when things go wrong
During the night and day time too
I bow my head and sing my song
And the light comes shining through

    There are times when things are fair
    And we go about our way
    Acting like we just don't care
    About anything-come what may

There are times when things go well
And we don't thank him as we should
Neither do we ever tell
Of the goodness that we could

    Well I'm telling JESUS is the answer
    The life, truth and the way
    JESUS is the answer anytime
    And he'll lift you everyday.

JESUS

Jesus removed my cares
    He took them all away
Jesus just enfolded me
    He said he'll walk with me today
Jesus held me when I cried
    And my weeping eyes he dried
Jesus told me that with me
    He will always stay
Jesus lifted my burdens
    And showed me what to do
Jesus just surrounded me
    With friends like HIM and you
Jesus walked my path today
    Jesus told me what to do
And my Jesus showed me
    I must minister to you.

Since God has been
    Guiding my footsteps
I walk a little straighter
      If I stumble . . . he catches
    Fall . . . he lifts
      There is no one greater.

SIDE TITLED POEMS

TO MOTHER WITH LOVE

There are times that I remember
Of you tucking me in bed-and I've

Memories of those moments
Of you kissing my forehead
Thoughts of you beside me
Hearing me say my prayers
Every night was something different-even
Remembrance of your care.

Well I think you now know
I copied what you did I
T tucked my son in tight-and
Heard him say his prayers each night.

Learning how to pray
Often helps us later on-cause
Victory over death occurred
Each time I prayed a psalm.

I AM SO LONELY

I sit and think about my life

And know I should be someone's wife
Making a house into a home

Sharing instead of being alone.
"Oh Dear GOD, please hear my plea

Let a good man come to me
One who'll set my heart aglow—and
Naturally allow our love to grow
Especially since I want to give
Literally all—for I want to live.
You know it's not good being alone

In search for a love of your very own

And as I sit and reminisce
Most thoughts are of craving happiness

Some are sad—I let love slip by
One thought makes me sit and cry.

Loneliness is an ache so deep
One which makes you want to sleep
Namely to escape from pain
Escape from living lies again
Loneliness enters in your dreams
You can't help but toss and scream
         For it to give you peace of mind
         And leave you be some of the time."

BREAKTHROUGH

Before I saw you staring
Reaching out for me
Every one had angered me
Asking for a piece
Keeping time and keeping pace
Telling me their lies
Having the nerve to kiss my lips
Reminding me to my face
Only sex is what they want
Ultimately, it will be—if
God don't give me the anger I need—to
Holler——leave me be.

LOO K UP AND LIVE

Life is full of pleasant surprises
Often when your heart least expect them
One day a special one came my way and
Kept me from feeling life was dim.

Until them I was simply existing
Peace of mind was hard to find

And Jesus came within my heart
Now thoughts of him are in my mind.
Daily, I look up and pray

Listening just to hear his voice
I pay attention to what he say
Victory's mine for he's my choice.
Every since I heard the words
                "Rejoice in me, look up and live."
                Fullness of joy is what I receive.
                Understanding and love are what I give.

DEPRESSION

Depression-sadder-discouraged
Emotionally-low in spirit
Particular since I allowed myself—to
Repress the feelings and know it
Each day I have felt
Sadden—and even full of pain
Simply cause I felt you see,
I can't reach where I aim
Oh but now the time has come—to
Never feel this way
        For I've made up my mind
        To be uplifted, everyday.

FORGET

From sun up to sun down
Or from dusk to dawn
Reminisces from the past
Goes with me all day long
Even though I'm trying hard
To forget it all
        I find I must forgive
        and you must forget to call
First I fell upon my knees
Oh GOD, I prayed aloud
Remove the thoughts I think of
Get me out of this cloud
Enveloping me, it is full of sin
Thank you for hearing my plea
        I will forgive, I will forget
        Thank you for helping me.

PERFECTION

Peace
Encouraging me to live,
Radiates brilliance when I
Forgive.
Everything is finally
Calm,
Thank God
I'm willing to go on.
Once I thought so negative
Now I don't since I forgive.

SENSITIVITY

Sometimes people look at me
Envying my portrayal
Noticing all that they can see
Sensing my betrayal
In time when their eyes meet mine
They look and then they stray-and
I feel they want me and my time-by
Visiting me each day
I cry because I'm sensitive—about
The thoughts they think
Yet my mind is inquisitive
            And so with them I drink
            But I'm the captain of this ship
            I navigate my soul
            I'm the crew which back my lips
            I protect my being whole.

DO HAVE MERCY, HONEY

Don't ever leave me all alone
On a star lit night, sitting at home

Have mercy dear, come home to me
And let me sit upon your knee
Very soon—I'll change your mind
Ever wonder when we do spend time
about
My feelings constantly being hidden
Even denying the love that's usually given
Reaching out—but was denied
Crying tears—I usually hide
You look at me and shake you head
Have a drink and go to bed
One day soon you'll realize
Nothing but love was in my eyes
Eventually honey, you'll see
You lost my love by neglecting me.

SENSATIONAL

Since GOD reached out and shared my pain
Emanating from my heart
Now I find I'm not the same
Since we've been apart
All the hurt I felt within
That caused me misery
Instantly came to an end
Only cause GOD set me free
Now I go about my days
And I do so with ease
Learning how to change my ways
                For it is GOD I will please.

LET 'S GO IN 88

I want you to know something

Love, I love you so
Of all the things I say and do
Very soon I think you'll know-
Each time that I am with you

You ease my troubled mind
One time, especially, we loved
Until we both were fine.

I need you to come over

Knock lightly on my door
Next take me in your loving arms
On the bed or on the floor.
Whenever problems arise

Always feel free to speak, or

Go away to think it
Over, then return my dear and you'll see-that
One thing I love is peace of mind
Don't ever deny us the chance

To work things out for we deserve—to
Have a good romance.
I love you in a tender way
Now you're my every thing
God above has blessed our love and

We deserve to sing.
Having others see-what love has done
Even share our happiness
Now that we share our life as one

I know that we've been blessed.

Some people will look upon us—and
Question what we share, but
Understanding that we'll overcome
Every problem—cause we care.
Each day when we awaken
Zeal lodge within our hearts—for
Each of them know—we'll always be—and

I believe we'll never part.
To go through life and finally have

Love enter in our life
Even though we'll have ups and downs
There will never be any strife.
Sweetheart, don't you know by now

God meant for us to be—we're
Overcoming every obstacle

Including marriage—you see.
Now we should share between us

8 virtues to succeed—and all
8 mean a lot you see—for we were meant to be.

ON ANY GIVEN DAY, I AM A V.I.P.

One night I went to hear some jazz—and
Noticed people staring at me. I

Asked my girlfriend did I look bad. She said
No, you're glowing radiantly.
Your face portrays a thing of beauty.

Glowing cheeks and eyes which flash.
I think you look about ten years younger.
Very attractive—full of class.
Everything about you draws attention—even
Now while we sit and talk.

Did you notice how you gracefully sit
And how you glide when you walk?
You even set the atmosphere—and

I've noticed you're admired by all

And I enjoy being out with you
My dear, I've simply had a ball."

As time went by I couldn't help but notice

Various people coming over to me
Introducing themselves, giving compliments—like
Phyllis, you are a V.I.P.

DARRYL BUTCHER I LOVE YOU

Deep within my heart I know-I'll
Always want and love you so
Really I look forward to-and
Readily share my time with you
Your time you share is really good
Love, I never thought I could

Be as happy as I've been
Usually, cause I'd be just a friend
Take time you need to know me well
Cause my love, you can never tell
How much our love could really grow
Eventually, you will finally know
Reasons why our love should be

I hope one day that you will see
Love between us is so nice-and
Only this love will suffice
Very soon you'll finally know-that
Evidently, I love you so

You'll look at me with realization
Only I love you, with no hesitation
Until that day, I want you to know

         I love you so, and I won't let go
         For our love was meant to be
         And this is what the whole world see.

DARRYL BUTCHER

Deep in my heart, feelings for you grow
And this I think you already know
Remembrance of the times we share
Really make me deeply care
You opened my eyes and made me realize
Life has a lot to offer as time pass by.

Between us we've experienced such joy
Ultimately others will try to destroy
The beauty of your every touch-I find I
Cherish oh so much
Here's what I'm wishing in my heart
Eventually, that you'll begin to start
Reaching out and showing you care
      to spend as much time as you can spare.
      So **DARRYL BUTCHER** I hold out my hand
      And I want you to know that I understand
      That right now you want to be more than a friend
      And I'll accept that to no end.

BIBBY

Beautiful people are a rarity
I find as I go through life—the
Bulk of them are taken
But they still suffer strife.
You know one day, I asked for a

Beautiful person to be sent my way.
I found that all that glitters is not gold
Because of certain words he said.
But I still felt my day would come
Yet I couldn't help but wonder when.

But when that rarity came my way
I was better to him than a friend.
Beautiful moments were spent together
Beautiful times were shared
Yesterday's memories were forgotten

Because we made a beautiful pair.
I'm glad I looked forward to that day—for
Bill is who I know I desired and
Bibby—he is somewhat like
You—a rarity who inspire.

CALVIN MARSHALL

Can I share with you how I feel
Acknowledging all I feel within
Let me show you it's for real
Very soon, my beloved friend.
It's growing with words left untold
Naturally each and every day

Making feelings spread within my soul
And enjoying it in every way.
Recently, you wrote to me
Sharing what you felt within
Having no idea that I could see
And knowing I didn't want it to end.
Let's let our friendship continue to grow.
Let's throw all caution to the wind.
       I think in the end we'll both know—
       The joy of a love that should never end.

ROBERT SIMMON S-PAL

Recently, I met you
On a Friday night
Bobby introduced us and
Every since that night-I
Reminisce about you
Telling myself yes

Somehow I want you as a friend cause
I deserve the best.
Many times I think of you
My mind won't let it be—we were
Only ships out in the night
Not knowing what would be.
Since Bobby introduced us—

Please be just a friend
Always dealing with respect
Let's do that till the end.

BOBBY GRANT WELLON S-MY FRIEND

Before I met you—I can say
Others led my life astray
But I know that I'm to blame
Because I failed to use my brain.
You entered my life as a friend

Giving support to the very end
Reaching out and letting me know
Another path would please me—so—
Now I know just what you mean
The peace flows in a constant stream.

Why? Because I feel at ease
Enjoying myself, and I feel pleased—in
Learning to bowl and other moments shared
Letting you show a friend does care.
On some days I look back and smile
Not knowing I just walked a mile
Sharing it with a friend so dear

Mindful you'll always be near.
You know I think we'll always be

Forever close—and I can see—that
Really from the very start
Inside of you is an open heart.
Exceptionally warm and partially true
Now I no longer feel so blue.
Dear friend, I'm glad you're in my life
              And since you are, there's little strife.
              Continue sharing everything,
              So I can enjoy the joy it brings.

I HAVE BEEN WAITING

I have been waiting oh so long

Honey—you just don't know—I was
Always waiting with
Virtues—for an
Everlasting love. It was

Blind to the obvious
Even though you told me so—and
Every day which passed me by, I questioned GOD above-I asked him to
Nudge me gently so I would know

When true love came my way
And let the love within me flow
Increasing more each day.
The time we've spent together
Increased the love within—and
Nothing will be held from you—I'll
Give until the end.

Still we have a way to go
Oh love, let's let it be

Let's allow the feelings we possess—grow
Oh so endlessly.
Nights, I sit and think of you
Giving me so much love

I reminisce about moments shared—and
Cry when I think of
All the times I had someone, but
Needed *you* by my side—and

Prior to us getting together—I
Realized you were my guy.
Oh honey, I have waited so long—so
Be with me always
And by *your* side please let me be and
By *my* side—please stay.
Let me give to you my love and
You give me the same—let's

Give each other everything-for we have
Everything to gain.
Take me in your arms today

And hold and squeeze me tight

Just rock me slowly and rock me gently
Over to the bed on our right.
Begin to kiss me tenderly

And let our passions build
Sweetheart, let's just share our joy

And desires dear let's fulfill

With warmth, with love, with passion
And all that we possess
I have been waiting oh so long—for
This love—joy—happiness.
Realize this, my dear
Ever since you've been away—I
Stayed at home and waited patiently—
Sugar—for this day.

I LOVE YOU BECAUSE YOU ARE VERY SPECIAL

I really love you dear because, your

Love has a hold on me
Often I find I think of
Various times we've shared.
Each and every day is new

Yet you fail to know
Of just how much I care for you
Unless you don't think so—

But because you have undying love and
Express the same each day
Carefully cultivating it
And yet leaving much unsaid
Until you find the time my dear—to
Share with me a bit more
Eventually, the love may wilt and

You'll walk out the door.
Oh honey I want so very much—for
Us to always be

And I want you to treasure—the
Right for you and me—to
Enjoy days as they go by

Visually showing the love
Each of us feel-and express—but when
Reaching out—let's try—
Yielding to each other

Sharing the good and bad
Picking up each other's moods
Especially if we're sad.
Certainly dear, you're special.
I know you know it now.
Although it's kind of shaky
Love, we'll have our ups and downs.

BE MY LOVE

Many time I have wondered, whether love would come my way.
If so would I recognize it, or push the love away.
The times we've spent together, caressing tenderly
And looking in each others eyes, often come to me.

Even your voice moves me, especially over the phone
Makes me wish that you were near, instead of me being alone.
Looking at you longingly, aching for your arms
To wrap me oh so tenderly, today and all night long

Longing hard to taste every morsel of your lips
And wanting oh so very much to be beneath your hips.
Honey, I'll be myself. Darling, just for you
For I want truth to be involved, with everything I do.

Every since I met you realization settled in
That I must have you in my life as more than just a friend.

Be the one I lean on
Each and every day
      And you in turn can lean on me
      when things don't go your way.
My dear, I really need you
You're the man who I think of
      and even though we're far apart
      I'm filled with so much love.
Longing just to hold you
On this winter night—hoping oh so patiently—that things will be alright.
Very soon, my dear I feel
Each day will bring us joy—because we'll actually share some time
      to love each other more.

PRESCRIPTIONS FOR LOVE

Please share your passion and joy
Release to me forever more
Ecstasy granting relief and
Sweetness that's beyond belief
Cherish the moments we share
Relinquish the love that you bear for
I want you to feel happiness and
Pain of too much tenderness.
The love which gives you sorrow gives joy
Igniting desire for more
Often when I long for love
Naturally it's you that I think of.
Surely you feel much the same

For true love is not a game
Oh darling please share love with me
Reach out and take me tenderly.

Love me whether right or wrong
Oh love me honey all night long
Very soon I'll give to you
Everything you prayed for too.

PRESCRIPTION FOR LOVE

Pity me baby for I'm strung out over you
Reaching out constantly
Expecting to be held by you
Since you're not here I
Continuously cry the blues
Release me from this misery or
I'll get my freedom from you.
Pity me baby; take this love I'm giving you
Take all you can, but take it all from me.
I will give you happiness and comfort too
Oh dear just love me and let us be.
Now that you've got me darling, forget the past

Forget old times, for our future darling will last.
Oh honey please be my prescription for love
Relieve me from my misery with all you think of.

Let all this pain that I feel within
One day cease, as our love begin.
Visualize the happiness we'll
Eventually share   Be my prescription for love, darling if you dare.

5th PRESCRIPTION

I've got a pain in my heart I've had it since we've been apart
I'm feeling lonely feeling blue feeling depressed with nothing to do
I'm always crying I'm alone waiting here patiently by the phone
Honey, it's you I'm thinking of constantly pleading for your love.
I'm also pleading to God above I need a prescription for lost love
In order to make me feel as I should I'm going to see Dr. Feelgood
Unless you want to take this pain that is driving me insane

> **P**lease come back to me
> **R**elease me from my misery
> **E**very since the day you left—it
> **S**eems loneliness won't let me be. I am
> **C**rying all night long
> **R**eally missing you now that you're gone
> **I** am pleading constantly for a
> **P**rescription for love.
> **T**ell me you still want me
> **I**n your life and that you'd be
> **O**nly my prescription for love and
> **N**ow you'll give me relief

To this pain within my heart
That I've had since we've been apart
I was crying feeling pain
Until the day you finally came

> And healed my heart
> With a brand new start

But I am still lonely
But I'm no longer feeling blue
Cause I've discovered
That I really don't need you.

PROVE TO YOU I LOVE YOU

Prove to you I love you, is what you asked of me
Really, all I wish to do is just let our love be
One should never have to ask if the love exist
         and never have to question joy and happiness.
Visualizing answers have really let me know
Every since the day we met, I have loved you so.

Tonight you caused me to reflect and admit I know
Of the feelings I possess for you which causes the outer glow.

You know you're the one for me and our love should be
One of warmth and closeness—that we share happily.
Usually I shed tears of joy—this *you* don't know

I don't know how I can prove how much I love you—so

Likewise, I don't think *you* know
Of the love you have for me
Very deep within you—but you'll find it won't let you be.
Even though you claim you care

You still aren't being fair—for you won't
Open up your eyes and see—your
Unboundless love for me.

A SPECIAL NOTE TO THANK YOU

A short time ago—I was alone

Sitting patiently by the phone
Praying desperately for a call
Especially from whom I gave my all.
Changes are happening in my life
I now can feel peace instead of strife
And I feel I owe it all to you
Let me thank and love you too.

Never have I felt like this
Often I sit and reminisce—about
The calls I receive from you
Expressing things that we could do.

Thank you love for giving me
One last chance to try to be

That positive person I feel with
Happily changing with a friend.
A special prayer is being prayed
Not just right now, but everyday.
Knowing with **HIM** and you being near

Yes, I can finally stop the tears.
Once upon a time—I cried—it was
Usually cause—I denied
        me being myself and it caused me pain
        but because of you—I smile again.

WISHING YOU WERE HERE

When I awaken this morning
I stretched my arms out wide
Searching fingers reaching out
Hoping you were by my side
I opened slowly swollen eyes
Noticing again——that you were
Gone—I was alone

Yet my heart still sang
Once it bothered me when you left
Usually I felt sad

Well now I cry no more my love
Except when I am glad
Reaching out, my dear for you
Excites me oh so much

Happily I write a tune
Expressing love and such.
Really honey, I'm aching
Especially since you're gone
        Knowing I'll be here all day
        Alone, till you come home.

I Need YOU Darling

I promise to keep you

Now if you want me to
Even if you later
Exit, and leave me feeling blue.
Dearest, I'll treasure

Your deeds I cannot measure
Only you are my man
Usually, you're my pleasure.

Dearest, men will daily try—to
Attract me from you
Really they don't know that at
Least—that's the one thing they can't do
If heaven has blessed us
Now especially with trust—I
Guess we should no longer fear
             we won't make it for we must.

SPECIAL

Someone looked within my eyes and
Peeped within my soul
Expected me within his life and
Caused my heart to glow
Immediately, because we knew
Always the love would flow. The
Love was special between us two
        For we shared a special glow.

BEAUTY

Being here beside you
Engrossed in what's being said
Awaken thoughts within me
Unconscious during the day
Today, I sit and reminisce
Yesterday's hurts and pains
        But tomorrow holds the promises
        of what a new day will bring.

SPARKLE

She closed her eyes to go to sleep
Pretending that she did not need
Anyone to hold her tight
Regretting that they had a fight
Kindness grew within her great
Lighting her up with radiance
Especially since you took her hand
        and told her, "darling let's try again."

SOFTNESS

Sinking ever so tenderly in your loving arms
On the sofa, chair or bed or even on a farm
Feeling the softness of your hair, the tenderness of your touch
Tasting the sweetness of your lips and wanting you so much
Needing to feel the warmth we share and the closeness too
Enjoying more knowing you care about everything we do
Sharing the softness of our love gently enveloping our hearts
Sharing the strength within our minds, knowing we'd never part.

BENEFITS

Being in love is beautiful
Especially if it's true
Now or later, I'll have mine and
Eventually not feel blue
Friends continuously call me
Inviting me to come out
Telling me I'm missing fun
Shouting all about.

But deep within some of their hearts
Envy's what they feel
Never the less I don't mind
Enjoying being for real
For I know I feel no shame
In me being myself, and
That's a benefit I'll enjoy-while
Staying true to myself.

LIFE IS A TRAGEDY FULL OF JOY

Looking out the window
I find I feel perplexed
For life is just a tragedy
Every one admits to next

I'm finding out while traveling through
Such is the same for me

And I don't know just what to do

To deal with tragedy.
Recently, I think I found
An answer to deal with
Giving joy to whom I'm around
Evidently is a gift—to
Deal with life
You must realize—it can be

Full of joy—don't allow anyone to
Use you—for your
Life is not a toy.
Life is a tragedy——full

Of ups and downs
Fortunately, for some of us

Joy helps keep us sound.
Often I find just in time
You reap just what you sow
        So I will plant some happiness
        blessed with peace and joy.

HELL IS TRUTH SEEN TOO LATE

Hope lies deep within us
Even though I know
Love has often found me
Lack of it hurt me so

I sit back and constantly
Stare at stars above

Trying hard to understand
Reasons just why love
Usually escapes my grasp
Though I give so much
Hope within is empty

So I am in a rush.
Every since I met you
Each day I felt a glow
Noting everything we did

Things helping my love to flow
Only just to realize
One thing I should have thought of—was
            getting back with you and
            giving another try to love.
Love will again come my way
And you will appreciate
The feelings I offer to share
Each and every day.

WE'RE ALL IN THIS TOGETHER-BY OURSELVES

We've come this far together
Each of us holding on

Remembering we have far to go—as
Each night turns to dawn.

All of us have problems—making
Life hard to face
Love will lead us the right way

If we just keep pace.
No one knows the pain we feel

They don't know our shame
Heck, they don't even know the rules
If they play our games.
Some in which we hold inside

Thoughts which hurt us so—and
Once they do and feel our pain
Guilt will ride us more.
Each of us has faith
To whip what ails us now
Hope is never ending
Even though we frown.
Respect for one another

Brings about an inner glow
Yet we hold feelings in reserve—for

Our way is long to go.
Ultimately, we'll find ourselves
Reaching to someone
Sure, it hurts to reach halfway
Every one of us hurt-some.
Let us help ourselves-and
Very soon we'll see
Each of us will benefit
So why not let it be.

THE THINGS WE WANT IN THE WORST WAY

Searching oh so very long
Often for a love of
My own—caused me to live a lonely life—and have an
Empty life at home.
The times that I spent searching
Increased as years went by
My face was a sight to behold—for my
Eyes revealed I cried.
Sometimes it is better to have loved and lost

Then to never have loved at all
However, it's not always worth the cost—my
Experience was my downfall.

The few times I have experienced love
Have left me feeling perplexed
I've felt the joy—warmth—happiness
Now loneliness—how I ache!!!
God sent to me someone to love
Someone who loves me too

We spend time being together
Except the time is few.

We've accepted our relationship
And all the problems too
Now I find I must be strong
To solve one or two.

I want this man for I love him and
Need him in every way—for

The love he has been giving me
Has made me happy everyday.
Each time that we are together

We express the joy we feel
Of sharing a thing of beauty
Recognizing it's for real.
Still we both have problems—and
There's one we can't ignore

Which is the fact that he's married
And when he walks out the door—
Yes, he's going back home to his wife

And I am left alone
Really I've accepted it—for
Each place is his home.

This man who has come my way
Has made me want to live
Each and every day with him—for

We have lots to give. Not
Only to each other will we
Reach out and hold
Still we have to do our best
To solve problems still untold.

Previously, I went through life
Reaching out for love
Often settling for anything
Because of want of love.
Lack of love had made me feel
Emptiness within
My problem now is I'm alone—it
Seems I just can't win.

PEOPLE WITHOUT ANYTHING

Pretending everything is alright
Each one tell the lies
Of not having any worries—and
Problems they deny.
Liars, laughing, hard and long
Especially in a crowd

Without anyone to call their own
Insisting they are not loud.
They drink their booze, their beer, their wine
Have drinks sent to everyone
Of course they'll ask you out to dine
Usually, to prolong their fun.
They get upset if you decline

And then they end up mad
Now you must remind them of their lies
You must—or end up sad.
They tell you they don't worry
However, they get on you.
If you say no—you've no hurry-you've
Nothing else to do.
Guess what, they'll try to knock you

They ask why are you there.
Of course you smile—hold up your head and
Whisper softly in their ear—
Oh you're just out to socialize
Relax and forget your woes—for
Really you have worries—but
You don't deny them—so

After you put them in their place
Be silent and reflect
On what you did throughout the day and
Upon what you will do next.
The next thing you will hear is

"Are you really in deep thought?
Really nothing is worth worrying about,
Especially if it can be bought."

Gracefully, you raise your eyes
Enjoying what you'll say next
Not caring how they react
Especially if you have an ache.
Really, (his is how you begin)
Are you addressing me?
Let me tell you short and sweet
Liar, please leave me be.
You run your mouth, you talk real loud

Of you not having worries
Now you're in my face—minding my biz and
Telling dirty stories.
Here, have another drink
Evidently, you need one and
I want you out of my face—also I
Really don't want you or your slimy embrace.

Well, what are you waiting for?
Are you thinking about your lies
You said you had no worries yet you

*T*ake my harsh replies.
*O*h I see you are on your way

*T*o the cemetery nearby—by
*H*aving your drinks one after another—you
*E*ven have tearstained eyes.

*C*ut out all the foolishness—go
*E*at a hot square meal
*M*ake up your mind to cut out the booze
*E*ven try being for real.
*T*hat graveyard is not too far away
*A*nd you are heading for it
*R*eally, try to give your liver a break—and
*Y*our worries, try to admit.

WAITING IN VAIN FOR LOVE FROM YOU

When I came home from work tonight
All I looked forward to
If I may take the time my dear—and
Tell this thing to you
I was looking forward to sharing time
Not caring about the weather—and
Glowing very deep within

In knowing we'd be together.
Now I know I was oh so wrong—and

Very soon I'll admit the same
About me being a fool for you and
In love being just a game.
Never have I felt this way

For I'm feeling so mixed up
Over wanting time you spare for me and
Really dear, I messed up—in

Letting love you feel for me
Overwhelm me to the point—of
Virtually blinding me to
Everything—and causing me to smoke a joint.

Forever, I will feel this way—so
Really I've one last chance
Of taking control of my life by
Maybe forgetting about romance.

You gave me feelings I've never known
Of true love and happiness
Until I felt tonight, that you, my love, could really care less.

LONELINESS IS A BITCH

Love, you've stood me up
Over and over again
Never once did you call
Each time I waited in vain
Looking back, I realize now
I was just a fool
Needing you so desperately
Expressing love so true
Since then dear, I realize how
Silly—how stupid I was

In wanting and expecting
Sweetheart, you—your time—your love

And as I wipe my tear stained eyes

Baby, you ought to know
I deserved just what I got
Thanks for the final blow
Crying will not ease my pain—nor end my loneliness
However, I can say again—loneliness is a bitch.

IMPOSTER

I love you dear
More than you'll know
Please take a chance
Once more or blow
Something special
That could have been shared
Even though *you* don't
Remember *I* care
about the things we say and do
about my time I share with you
especially since you do not care
and especially since you're not being fair.
I won't hurt long
My dear you'll see
Please don't feel guilt—for
One day I'll be
Someone special
To someone new
Enjoying my life
Remaining true
To that new love—until *he* find
he doesn't want me—but he'll be kind
in telling me he loves me so
but because of age—he's letting me go
But I will find an older man
And be with him as long as I can.
The pain, hurt and loneliness will cease
When the love I share with a loved one increase.

CONDITIONS

Could you ever hold me tight
On a long, cold lonely night
Now I think I'd want you to
Darling, hold me close to you
If you know I yearn for you
Take me, let me-hold you too
Immediately, I'll feel alright
Only if you hold me tight
Next I want a tender squeeze
Smothering me-increasing my needs
   Kissing gently on my ear
   Fingers rippling through my hair
   Throbs, I feel everywhere
   With you showing that you care
   Because my dear, you feel at ease
   In knowing that I'm easily pleased.

EMERGENCY

Every since the day we met
My life hasn't been the same
Each day I face and
Realize—that I am to blame—in
Giving you so much freedom—to
Enjoying me when you wished—and
Not seeing me when you
Could—so instead I reminisce
You must be more considerate—in dealing with me
   You must because it's now become a dire emergency.

ANTICIPATION

As I sit here waiting
Not knowing if you really care
Time is dragging by oh so slow
I'm counting minutes one by one
Couldn't you have at least called me
Instead of making me wait like this
Presuming that you'll soon be here
And hoping that I don't miss
The sound of you knocking
Intensely, at my door
Oh darling, hurry home to me
Now and forever more.

MARRIAGE

Many years ago, we shared a dream. We shared our life as a perfect team.
As the years passed, we began to doubt, fuss and fight, suffer and shout.
Reality opened up our eyes and we began to realize
Respect for each other was dying fast, and our relationship wasn't going to last.
Instead, somewhere down the line we opened our eyes to leave behind
All the pain we suffered-problems we shared and unite as one because we cared
Guess what, we're experiencing it again, only this time I can't bear the pain
Eventually, my love, I'll get rid of this ache . . .

for by us getting married-we made a mistake.

DAMAGED

Dutifully, I hold my breath
Awaiting your next word
Maybe it will stay within
And let *me* be heard
Giving you my very best
Even though I'm tired-of
Doing all which you expect
                Feeling uninspired.

Dear, you know you're selfish
And you broke my heart
Maybe soon it'll go away
And we will finally part
Go on my dear and leave me be
Even though it'll hurt
Darling, I'd rather be alone
                Than to live with your dirt.

PLASTIC PEOPLE

Praising all material gains
Laughing all about
And haven't got a pot to pee or
Shit-yet
They loudly shout
Insisting they have plenty
Cash

Pretending they have fun
Eventually they finally admit-truth
Of being alone
Pride goes out the window
Lies replaced by truth—and
Even then, they don't realize
                They are of little use.

PAIN

Sometimes I feel so afraid
Sometimes I sit and stare
Sometimes I feel so much pain
Cause I have no one who care

P—is for my patience
A—anxiety
I—must also admit
N—is for my need.

Hurt-Pain -Sensitivity

Honey, I really want you—but don't
Use me for I care
Really I'm beginning
To not even fear

People hurting me constantly
And casting me aside
Including you, my dear sweetheart
Not wanting to be only *my guy*

Sometimes I sit and wonder
Exactly what I did—but
Nothing comes to mind
Since you walked out instead
I sit, I read, I write
This to use my time
I dream, I hope, I pray
Vigorously, for peace of mind
I know that soon my day will come
To stop my search for love
You see, I'm becoming a realist
              because I've had enough.

LOVE, LOVE, LOVE

Living life so gingerly
Oh, if only you knew, that
Very deep within me
Each day is sort of blue

     Life offers nothing to me
     Or let me take from it, and
     Very soon, I'll cease
     Existing, for I know I'm sick—of

          Looking for my peace of mind
          Of searching high and low
          Virtually feeling out of time
          Eventually dying alone, I know.

Can
Love
Erase
All
Negatives

Thoughts
In
Me
Exploding?

Sometimes
Thoughts
Remembered
Eventually
Nullify
Giving
The
Heart.

DECEASED ONES

IN REMEMBRANCE OF MY FIFTH GRANDSON, CAMERON,

in a week was killed, on my front door steps.
4/30/21 was for real,
and is a pain for us all from the depth.

4/30/21 is your new birthday,
the date of your entrance into heaven you see.
But in our hearts you'll continue to live
for we'll always have you as a memory.

My son, his mother and the rest of us know
that ALLAH has you in His arms
and we know you are truly safe
from any additional pain, suffering or harm.

painfully written by his grandmom Umi aka Phyllis Ames Bey

THE ROLE MODEL- CONSTANCE M. JOHNSON

Connie continuously stayed constant in keeping us on the right track
Only allowing us to operate with integrity and tact
Never did she stray her life's journey path
Surely ABBA FATHER welcomed her home because of that
The dignity and personality of my friend was heart warming
And the way she communicated was very charming
Now when I did not here from her for a month and a half
Connie stayed on my mind, I shed tears and a laugh
Eventually, we all found out what happened to her

Mainly, because her demise occurred

Just let thoughts of her love for us exist
On any day or night that we feel she is missed
Have thought of our love for her as we reminisce
Nice times or moments when we make our list
Sharing thoughts of her sharing with us our world
On her being our mother, sister or our girl
Never ever have we had such a very good friend
          and she was really this until the end.

Past events and conversations keep her alive
in our hearts and minds as we continue to strive
to accept that our Connie has ascended
so let us stop thinking life has ended
She has everlasting life with God above
He called her home to experience divine love.

By phyllis ames-bey and Saleem E. Ali-bey

TANYA BUTCHER-6/11/08

*T*anya, if you only knew
A lot of people loved you.
*N*ow, I bet you really don't know—
*Y*ou know we are sorry you had to go.
*A*nother day has come and gone

*B*ut your memory lingers on
*U*sually, we were filled with joy
*T*oday we are not—that was before
*C*ancer took you away from us
*H*owever, we really cannot fuss
*E*ternity in heaven now awaits you
*R*est in peace, whatever you do.

THE FRIENDSHIP OF LOVE-NIGHT LIFE BARNE Y

Love comes and goes in various stages—but when it's pure—it last forever.
I've known such a love—now I'm enraged—cause I've lost the presence of
A beautiful brother. When he was here—he gave me love as a father, a
brother, An uncle-a friend. Now that he's gone—though things have
changed, I'll still Love him until my end.

When times were bad and I felt blue and felt I had no where to turn
He made me smile and pulled me through and taught me what I had to
learn.
When I met love, Barney stood by me and showed me the man who I needed
I'm glad I took the time to see, because I found out he was indeed.

So though Barney has passed away
He gave to me a precious gift
He left me love that's here to stay
He gave to me a love which lifts.

Because he saw within my heart
Something which I tried to hide
He saw it from the very start
But now I finally realize

Before I seek love of a man
I should seek the love of a friend
One who is close, true and understand
That friendship is where love begins.

CLIFTON

Clift? I don't know where he is
    I don't know where he's gone
        If he's up among the stars
            Or if he is still alone

Why didn't he reach out to Joe
    Why didn't he take the time
        To call-or sit—and talk with Joe
            To ease his troubled mind

Sometimes Joe sit and wonder about
    The good times that they shared
        And wondered why Clift shut him out
            When he knew that he was there

To ease his mind—to share his pain
    To show him someone cared
        Did he think life was just a game
            Or that life was unfair?

Why didn't he reach out to Joe
    Why didn't he just say
        A little help was all he need
            On that very day

That day he just would not voice
    How he felt inside
        Instead he made a selfish choice
            Of committing suicide.

Clift? I don't know where he is
    Or if his mind is at ease
        If he is up among the stars
            Or finally feeling peace.

BOBBY

Bobby, if you only knew
Of how much you're being missed
By someone that you left behind
Before joining God above.
You every so often cross Steve's mind

But sometimes it causes him pain
Once in a while he reminisce
But he wishes you were here again
Bobby, oh Bobby, you are truly missed
Yes your memory lingers on

But they are memories of the good times shared
Of moments long gone.
But I told Steve, I'd write this poem
But my words cannot express
Your best friend heart filled with love,
Joy, sorrow, pain and happiness.

ASSOCIATES

TO MR. NHAMBUI

You've made me aware, and admit I'm unsure
And question why some things happen in the world
And because of you sharing your time with me
I'm able to see things more positively.
>You've made me aware by mesmerizing me
>You've made me aware cause I've allowed myself to be
>By your story-of the footprints in the snow
>It made me look inward and recognize and know
It's the innocent children who really suffer
In order for me to learn my problems are rougher
You've made me aware—and I bet
You haven't really weighed the situation yet
>But when and if you ever do
>Notice my esteem and assurance were raised by you
>I treasure the passing moments we have shared
>I even treasure the fact that you care
And for the present I foresee no complications
When I take a look at our situation
I love the time you spent listening
It made the hope within me really glisten
>It made me face up and notice no matter what we do
>It can only be friendship between us two
>I treasure your concern and your tender touch
>To me it really meant so very much
To find I'm not as bad as I thought
And realize affection doesn't have to he bought
I am that child within the snow
And I oh so really want to know
>Why must I always pay the price
>For adults to grow up, wise up and be nice

SL-I LOVED YOU AS A SISTER

It is better to have loved and lost—than to never have loved at all
That is what you always say—every time you call
But it's worst my dear to love someone and that someone doesn't love
you
To the same degree which you possess—so there goes your happiness
    It's worst my dear to love someone and they don't recognize
    The love you feel within your heart and reveal within your eyes
    It is worst when you're together and one of you feel alone
    And you reach out to ease the pain—and all they do is moan
Holding feelings deep with-shutting out your love
Crying on the inside while praying to God above
For him to ease the burden—make the burden light
Do whatever is necessary to make everything alright
    And in response God gave them love of one *friend* for another
    In response God gave her love of *sister* for a *brother*
    Yes, it is better to have love and lost than to never have loved at all
    And I'll remember that my dear—the very next time you call.

IN MEMORY OF AUGUST

On 8/11/1983
   Something wonderful happened to me
I met a man name Mr. LaNair
   Who showed me that he really cared
But I had to give him up you see
   Cause he didn't really belong to me
Cause he had a wife and also two kids
   And had but so much time to give

On 8/3/1984
   I experienced the joy once more
With a man I'll just call A.D.
   He made me feel I could be free
To be myself and enjoy life
   For there's more to it than stress and strife
But still I feel lonely with
   Cause I want him only as a friend

On 8/10/1985
   I met Wilson and I wanted to cry
He had characteristics of the previous two
   I felt distressed and then felt blue
For we were on a double date
   He, to meet my friend-and she came late
But in 86—I had him
   And he answered my every whim.

BIG DEAL

8/19 of 82—is one date
    I will never forget
I met you—though it was fate
    And I have no regrets
8/19 of 82—you took away
    My loneliness
With all you do—in every way
    I feel true happiness.

Big deal!!! It's a new one!!!!
    Damn near-every August
And every new start
    which began that month
Ended in a bust

But, when my divorce comes through
    I'll try again in April
Yes, that's when I'll start anew
    I will, with my friend Will.

MY GRIP

My grip is as the brightest lamp
    Holding you so light
My grip is like the strongest clamp
    It will hold you tight
My grip is soft and tender
    Caressing and so sweet
My grip will make you-love-surrender
    When per chance we meet
My grip will cling to you so tight
    But what am I to do
When I feel all we have is right
    Shared between us two
My grip can hold you in between
    A hold that's light or tight
My grip no matter what it seem
    Will make you feel alright.

CONF USING SEX WITH LOVE

I knew tonight, when the man said thanks
I was used for sex within his banks
I felt degraded—I felt ashamed
And I know I am the one to blame

I have no one to call my own
And I'm to blame for being alone
When I need sex—I pick men up
When people talk—I don't give a fluck

I'm flesh and blood—warm and alive
And take care of my needs—talking jive
I laugh outwardly and cry within
For I'm shame of living in sin

My arms ache to hold one man
My fingers ache to hold his hand
My body craves to be embraced
And my heart continuously race

To find someone to be my own
To hear his voice over the phone
To feel his lips just touching mine
I won't give up—it'll come in time'

LUST

There are some things one can't understand
I want to know why she wants to be a man
A friend of mine tried to hit on me
And I let her know it just can't be

She says she deals with a man of mine
And let me know she feels so fine
She's begging for time to try to blow
My mind—when she should really know

I have no time to roll that way
And don't have time to hear what's said
About the feelings she possess
Cause all I want is happiness

With a man I'll call my own
With hopes we'll share a happy home
But it takes time and it'll take love
Doing and sharing all we think of.

WHY WOMEN

Why am I attracting women to me
When I last went out—one touched my knee
Once, one reached out and tried to touch my hand
I simply laughed and said to her-I needed a man.
    Another wanted me oh so damn bad
    She asked my man could she get in bed
    Another came—into the bar
    Opened her blouse-her eyes roamed far.
A fifth kissed me upon the lips
Just sitting around waiting for me to slip
Let down my guard and be at ease
Waiting to do just as she pleased.
    Another rolls her eyes at me
    When she sees me with my man
    Wishing she was in his shoes
    Just aching to hold my hand
A seventh smiled and said there'll come a time
When I would want to make her mine
Another leaned over and exposed her breast
And then she asked me to unbutton her dress
    What women fail to realize
    When I look into my man's eyes
    It is only him who I desire
    And only he sets me afire.

BROKEN DATES

Smoothing out—cooling out—standing up everyone
Knowing full well it wasn't right—but it can't be undone
Lou—the camera man
Terry—the news reporter
Super Lou—Mr. Universe
Ron-the flashy sportier
Awbry waited long for our date
And Joe did also
Al forgot to reiterate
And so I didn't go
Joe made one for us to swim
Ron for us to smoke
Jim for a picnic
James for us to joke
I kept dates with James and Paul
And oh what misery
James begged me to go to bed
But I wanted Paul instead
Who wanted me to find someone
Single to share my time
But yet confessed his love for me
And of me being on his mind.

BREAKING UP

Breaking up is not hard to do when the time shared was few
We've had more good times than bad, that's why I won't be sad.
I don't have to love you anymore if you want to walk out the door
I won't want for you to call any longer-as I find I'm getting stronger
In ridding myself of my desire for you—I can play that game too
Go on your way—I wish you well—only time will surely tell
Whether it was a mistake on your part—to give me a broken heart
You set me as a seal upon you arm and failed to protect our love from harm

I believe you're cheating on me—you say you cannot be
You say you have time for no one but me-but you did it before you see.
I going to stop all my love for you—if it's the last thing that I do
The signs are there, you know it too—to this woman you can't be true
You took my picture off the wall—you failed to answer my calls
I gave to you my all and all—in love you made me fall
Another woman like me does not exist—you'll find out when you miss
My arms, my lips, my tender kiss—my legs and face you couldn't resist
But this is one thing I do know—I have to let you go
I really, really loved you so—but no longer will that feeling flow.

SUICIDAL THOUGHTS

GOD REALLY CARE

That's twice I looked for you
         To show through
But you didn't—so what am I to do
I'm sitting alone beside the phone
I'm at home thinking of you.
I'm also wondering constantly
Just what it is you see in me
I'm wondering just what do you expect
I'm also wondering what I'll do next.

I feel I'm no good for you
Just going by things I've done and do
For I'm on a self—destructive course
And can be stopped only by God's force.
I want to live-so desperately
With peace of mind-and happily
In country space with country air
And with someone who really care.

Pathetic

I MUST ADMIT THE FEELINGS WERE STRONGER
I DIDN'T WANT TO LIVE ANY LONGER
WITH THE PAIN, THE HURT, THE SUFFERING
WITH LIES, HALF TRUTHS AND OTHER THINGS.

     I USED TO ACHE SO WIDE, I USED TO ACHE SO DEEP
     I WONDERED HOW MUCH WITHIN ME I SHOULD KEEP
     I AM ONLY HUMAN AND AT TIMES FELT WEAK
     BUT THERE'S NO MORE PAIN WHEN I LAY TO SLEEP

I WON'T BEAR ANYMORE THIS I KNOW
AND THE FEW ACHES AND PAINS AREN'T KILLING ME—SO
GOD THANKS FOR HELPING ME, BEFORE IT WAS TOO LATE
FOR SUICIDE—WAS DANGLING BAIT

SYMPTONS

A person in crisis may be somatic
She may take an action which appears dramatic
She may feel isolated and try to take her life
Cause she's unable to deal with stress and strife.

Before removing herself from the situation
She may experience weight loss and irritation
Lower back pain or repeated injury
Hypo-and even hyperactivity.

Extreme fatigue—loss of appetite
Restlessness-tossing-turning through the night
Gall bladder or even ulcer attacks
Crying hysterically—over reacts.

I was somatic—this I realize
As I sit and wipe my tear-stained eyes
I know I thank God I didn't end my life
With pills, a car, gun, radio or knife.

WHAT 'S WRONG WITH ME

Projecting herself as nobody's baby
    As a whore or as everybody's maybe
Popping pills snorting dope
    All because she cannot cope

Drinking heavy dancing all night
    Loving rarely no lovers in sight
Give up thinking negatively
    Searching to find out who she is

Just what is the purpose of her life
    To be alone or some man's wife
I know it's trying I know it's rough
    But I'll hang in there I have to be tough

After awhile I'll be alright
    Cause I found a way tonight
I almost took an overdose
    Almost ended up becoming a ghost

There is only one thing I regret
    I've never experienced true love yet
So I'll be around for a while
    Until I learn to cope learn to smile

THINKING POSITIVE

The days go by so slowly
    My nights are twice as long
Because my self esteem is low
    And not up where it belong
The group I share my time with
    Has made me realize
Quality time darts by so swift
    And everybody cries.
But I become angry-I feel pissed
    When the staff whispers about us
I become alert so I won't miss
    Defending the group for I must
The staff workers have a lot of mouth
    They have a lot of time
They sucker you to open up
    Then say you're out of your mind
Now if I were really crazy
    I'd drop the radio in the tub
I would have had it turned on
    And would have definitely had it plugged
The days go by so slowly
    The nights still twice as long
But I no longer think lowly
    I just write poems and songs.

THE GROUP

"A" is such a quiet guy—afraid to open up
Afraid to express just what he feels—but his anger will erupt
"B" is such a sensitive one wanting love so much
Afraid to give but no one's worthy of his love-his time and such.
"C" opens up with the group but not in therapy
It seems as though they respect this and all just let him be.
"D" I feel a soft spot for because we've experienced the same
Too big of a responsibility placed on him was the game
"E" is such a vulnerable jewel-what she wants is love
But she needs to start being cruel and herself is whom she should think
of.
"F" is like a rose—but her thorns get in the way
Cause dear old dad has hurt her bad—still she'll be ok one day
Phyllis is the new one here. She's trying to go about
Getting her back together—instead of copping out.

"A" please find the courage to say just what you feel
Show all whom you meet or greet you'll be 100% real
"B" let go of the past and face reality
And you'll find life will become as you wish it to be.
"C" you seem so deep in thought—why not open up
Talk about what you know best—forget about the buts.
"D" it is too late for you-to be six years old again
Enjoy your life as an adult—enjoy the joy it will bring.
"E" you are so vulnerable and you have lots to give
So find a special new one so you can start to live
"F" please let someone help when they reach out their hand
Some of us know just how you feel—some of us understand
When "A" read the thought for today—I thought he spoke to me
In which one should go on living-if only to satisfy curiosity.

FOR WHAT?

"Show me what I'd be missing"
   Is what he said to me?
"Sometimes—I'm too smart for myself
   About what's suppose to be"
I look at him and wonder
   Just where he is coming from
I look at him and wonder why
   Our thing is being undone
Wondering about things
   Leaves a lot to be desired
Because thought have a tendency
   Of really starting a fire
One in which you're tempted to say
   "Dear God, just what's the use
Let ashes be ashes, dust be dirt
   Instead of being abused."
Oh, it could be so easy
   One could swallow pills
One could quickly pull a trigger
   It's only themselves they kill.

MY EULOGY

Just a touch of elegance
　　A touch of class per chance
When I'm finally laid to rest
　　Let me look my best.
Let the settings please portray
　　How I lived each day
One of joy scattered about
　　Whenever they saw me out.
Let it also please reflect
　　What I will say next
The emptiness I felt within
　　Even among my friends.
No one really knew me
　　No one understood
No one really accepted me
　　The way they really should've.
The pain I felt was oh so deep
　　Some lucked up and perceived
That I felt the way in which I did
　　For I gave all but just received—
Only all the negatives
　　Cause I felt I should be
Punished for my sins, my thoughts
　　Reactions and my deeds.

I AM TIRED

I have several friends—three times as many associates
    But have no one I can call my own—no one I can be with
I no longer feel so lonely—I no longer feel so blue
    'cause I've finally learned the difference—between loneliness and solitude

But then again somehow—whenever I reminisce
    I realize and admit—exactly what I miss
I miss being held in strong tender arms—throughout a dreary night
    A loved one's firm arms full of warmth—squeezing and wrapping me tight

On many, many occasions I had the opportunity
    To be some man's woman, some man's friend—companion or lady
But by the same token I realized I ran
    When they wanted a commitment of them being my man

I feel I ran because I didn't trust their words
    Their winking eyes, their quick actions—their ways and my nerves
Because I'm tired of being hurt—and feel I can't take no more pain
    Though a meaningful friendship just might be my aim

Really when I think of it—it strikes me as being funny
    Because everyone I met—cares about sex and money
If it's not either of those—then of a woman on their arms
    To make them feel and look real good—and dazzle others with her charms

I'm tired of feeling disillusioned, misused and abused
    I'm tired of coping with loneliness and even solitude
I'm even tired of men telling me I don't need anyone.
    Tired of thinking about suicide or being on the run.

THE EMPTY SHELL

Wanting someone here with you
    Wanting someone to share all you do
Feeling like a shell that's empty too
    Feeling very worthless in all you do
Wondering—why it is you exist
    Wondering what in life you have missed
Wondering if you'll ever fulfill your desires
    Wondering if he's yours and if you are his
Asking yourself if the day will come
    When you began to feel that you have done
Just about all that you can do
    Y et, your mate is still on the run
You began to feel you gave all you could give
    And wonder if you should continue to live
Feeling like an empty shell
    Or continue going on living a fib
I had a weakness called self-deception
    Causing self corruption and misconception
And the only way I felt I could be free
    Was by my own hand in self destruction

MY TEARS FOR STRENGTH

Why am I giving up on everything
    My home, my future, my life
Why can't I care 'bout what patience may bring
    Love, peace and joy, no strife
Why do I cry when the sun goes down
    Why do I cry when there is no one around
Why do I cry when the moon is aglow
    When the stars shine—cry with no sound.

Why is it whenever I meet someone
    They think I'm independent, pretty and smart
Why do they feel being around me is fun
    And fail to see the tears in my heart
Why do people tell me I don't need a man
    And make me feel they shouldn't hold my hand
Why does each of them fail to understand
    I don't wish to be as strong as I can.

No—I won't give up on anything
    Not even the dream of finding one who care
For one day soon my heart will sing
    Cause the burden from loneliness will cease being there
I won't shed any tears due to loneliness
    Though I would shed some due to happiness
They'll be tears for strength when I am weak
    From me fighting to continue to live.

THE LIVING DEAD

Walking around, feeling cold, but walking
    Numb, alone and unfeeling
Not giving a damn about themselves
    But to others—very yielding
Claiming they don't give a damn
    If they live or die
People around them look at them
    And sit and wonder why
But what the living don't realize
    Is dead souls wish to live
All it takes is a thing called love
    And they have lots to give
But not—if while giving
    They get nothing in return
Except the experience of being used
    And from this they quickly learn
It is better to be unfeeling
    It is better to be cold
Than to settle for feeling unloved and used
    And hurt by stories told.

I'LL BE AROUND

I used to sit, I used to cry
I used to always ask myself why
It seems I am destined to be blue
No place to go—nothing to do

I used to wonder if I died
Would my loved ones wish they'd tried
To make me feel all they possessed
The love, the joy, the happiness

I use to think of how it would be
If they would live life without me
Oh well, my thoughts aren't like that now
For I will always be around

WHAT 'S HAPPENING

What's happening, what's suppose to be
What does it take to deal with me
I'm vicious, cruel and calculating
Cold-blooded and procrastinating
I feel pain—I feel hurt
I cry in vain—from being treated like dirt
The man I thought I cared about
Doesn't call—and I feel shut out
He makes me feel he wants me here
For the convenience of being a dear
Maybe once or twice a week
other than that he doesn't speak
He told me just the other night
When I was standing to his right
You really know how to hurt a man.
He asked me to let go of his hand.
But he forgot he told me from the start
Don't fall in love, so I play the part
Of being happy—being glad
For I don't want him seeing me sad
So I put on a happy face
And act as though I know my place
But he doesn't know I'm dying within
In settling for just being a friend
I've gone as far as telling me
That being loved is not meant to be
So now I simply just exist
But in the end, I will be missed.

MY LYING PORTRAYAL

My past has been so lonely—full of hurt and pain
    Full of so much agony—loneliness and tears
My present hasn't been too well—it's really about the same
    Hurt pain and tears are still with me—during my current years
My future, I'm afraid to tell—I'm selfish but ashame
    Of planning to end this misery—but no one really hears
Me crying when I cry aloud—or see me reaching out
    No one understand me when I smile—or listen when I shout
I want to live—have love and peace-live in harmony
    I want to trust my life will change and end this misery
I'm tired of feeling lonely—tired of feeling depressed
    Being taken advantage of—or feeling I must impress
I'm fighting for my future—but how do I earn my trust
    Trust I will not hurt me more is definitely a must
Holidays are lonely times—you portray joy and such
    While all the time you cry within and hate so very much
Of feeling that you have to hide feeling so depressed
    But I'll continue for a while—for I feel I'm blessed.

YOU'RE MARRIED -YOU FAILED TO TELL HER

She has no one to hold her—no one understand
    Not even the one she squeezes tight
        And he's her only man
But then what difference does it make
    No one really cares—and all she knows is
        She is tired-of what she has to take
The one she's with had planned with her
    For her to be his wife
        Now she sits and wonders—if she should take her life
Because she's tired of all the games
    The beating around the bush
        No one wanting to be for real—and all are trying to push
Her mixed up mind to the edge—and she is shocked to find
    He mistrusted her and shut her out
        Of his arms, his heart and mind
Why? Exactly what's going on?
    Just what's suppose to be
        Is everyone just waiting to see her write her eulogy?
What's going on? Why doesn't she know?
    She suppose to be so smart
        Really she's dumb for trusting herself to open up her heart

WORTHLESS

When I pictured something blue
  I felt serenity
When I pictured something pink
  I knew I could think
About the past and present
  And the future too
Hoping that I'd always be
  Spending time with you
I see now that I was a fool
  To have such precious dreams
Of us always being together
  Of us being a team
Go ahead and kill myself
  It couldn't be any worst
Then living life all alone
  Having feelings of no worth.

IT'S NOT BAD

I AM OK—THIS I KNOW
  AND I'LL FEEL THE SAME—WHEREVER I GO
WITH A BRIGHT SMILE UPON MY FACE
  I'LL WALK ABOUT WITH JOY AND GRACE
SPARKLING EYES REFLECT THE GLOW
  I FEEL WITHIN BECAUSE I KNOW
I AM OK—IT IN MY VOICE
  I AM OK—I MADE THE CHOICE
TO BE JUST WHOM I WISH TO BE
  CAUSE IT IS NOT BAD IN BEING ME.

I WANT TO GO HOME

When people talk—I listen
    All the more carefully
Cause I don't know if what they're saying
    Actually refers to me
I felt my life in danger
    9/14/84
I feel the danger still exist
    And I'm frightened even more
Cause I don't know my enemies
    But I'm willing to let them be
All I want is peace of mind
    And them to let me be
I'm no danger—I'm no threat
    I don't even know their names
I don't know what they're about
    And I don't know their games
So why don't they just let me be
    Why don't they leave me alone?
I don't want a eulogy
    I just want to go home.

THE BELLS TOLLED

The bells tolled—the heads rolled
    The gossip flew among the crew
Who gives a damn except the few
    Who showed they cared and stuck by you
When the bells tolled and the heads rolled
    And you say, "WELL, COME WHAT MAY
I AM ALIVE, I DID SURVIVE
    I AM A PEARL IN THIS CRUEL WORLD
I AM AGHAST I LET THINGS LAST
    AS LONG AS THEY DID SINCE I WAS A GIRL
BUT NOW IT'S OVER—I WILL EXIST
    SOMEDAY—SOMEHOW—WHILE I REMINISCE
THE BELLS TOLLING—THE TONGUES ROLLING
    DYING SLOWLY AS I KEPT ON STROLLING."

SEARCHING FOR ANSWERS

Why is it I write so much
    About self destruction—love and pain
        Me wanting warmth and to be touched
Hiding from the sun—running in the rain
    Why is it I must play a role
        With man being dominate—me submissive
Why is it I do as I am told
    With him as the master-being permissive
        I can't and I refuse to continue to live—
My life as I have—the past few years
    And no longer shall I willingly give
        My all—and end up shedding tears.

DAYS-TODAY IS TUESDAY-I'M LOSING TRACK OF TIME

Little things—simple things—sets one off
Especially when subjected by those who think they know
Everything about you—running their mouth so
Because they see you constantly appearing to be on the go

They don't know themselves—yet they try to judge you
In whatever you say—and whatever you do
It's only one thing I want of them and that's to leave me be
Let them mind their own business and let me take care of me.

THE INNER ME-POERTY AND POEMS

CHANT —FOR INNER STRENGTH

Those who know me say they see
That there has been a change in me
The change is so conspicuous
It's caused a few of them not trust
    My happiness that I portray
    The joy I feel from day to day
    But most of them do feel at ease
    And tell me that they are really pleased
To see I've learned to live again
To see my joy instead of pain
To see my glow—to see my smile
To see my change has lasted a while
    I feel a lot of peace within
    My spirit will not let it end
    So I'll continue to express
    My peace—my joy—my happiness.
                    Cause (repeat 7 times)

MY EXPERIENCES

My happiest—having Saleem
   To give him all I feel I've missed
My saddest—getting credit
   I had enough to make a list
My loveliness—seeing loved ones
   Sharing news and having fun
My maddest—giving in
   Wishing to do what I should have done
My most peaceful—going to church
   Feeling forgiveness when I pray
My most bothersome—the job
   D read going back from day to day
My most sincerest—getting married
   Hearing him say I do
My most worrisome—his female friends
   Knowing they want him too
My warmest—feeling included
   When I see his relatives
My coldest—feeling shut out
   When I don't know what gives
My most precious—feeling loved
   Secured, peaceful and safe
My most painful—feeling abused misused
   Shut out and feeling hate.

UNTITLED

I AM A ROSE
   A RARE ROSE
      A BLACK ROSE
         A BEAUTIFUL ROSE
            WITH PETALS OF PORCELAIN
               SO FRAGILE
               MY WHOLE BEING
                  SMELLING
         WITH THE ESSENCE
         OF LOVE.
                  TASTING
         THE BRIGHT RAYS OF THE SUN
      BEAMING UPON ME
                  FEELING
         THE WARMTH
         GLOWING AND GROWING
   WITHIN ME
                  SEEING
         THE RADIANCE
         OF ITS LOVE
                  HEARING
         IT TELL ME OF
         THE BEAUTY, TENDERNESS AND SWEETNESS
      OF LOVE.
AND THE THORNS REMIND ME THEY ARE THERE ALSO, TO PROTECT.

EASILY AFFECTED

My protection is within the depths of my mind
There's a very high wall surrounding
vulnerable part. The wall surrounds my heart.
It has clinging vines growing upon it. As I look
around the wall, I noticed a section is beginning to
crumble. A ray of sunshine beams above, within
and through that hole.
    Shining
        Down
            Upon my heart
    Warming it
        Melting
            The ice
    The weathering of love
        Crumbling away the wall
    Ever so gently
        So tenderly
            So sweetly
    And I cry
        Silently
            Because my defense
                Was being torn down
                    Torn away
                        By love
Honey, I feel so vulnerable.

EXPOSED

Hard water—changed to ice
  Because of
    Neglect, coldness, lonesomeness
      And the feelings of
        Needing a hard protective shell
  So that the
    Softness, warmth and sensitivity
      Would not be vulnerable.
Icy,
  Not knowing or realizing
    The covering is not and was not
      Secure.
Ice,
  Cracking
    Breaking
      Into pieces
        From being to rigid
  Or melting
    From the warmth of love.
Either way—
  Your innermost self
    Is EXPOSED.

WES

Listening to Wes play
    Trying to portray
        Feelings of joy and tenderness
            But he has his way
In making one feel sorrow
    Making one feel depressed
        Because they have to hide
            Feelings of happiness
Wes can make you feel real bad
    Feel alone and sad
He can make you feel his joy
    He can make you glad.

WAS I LONELY?

In my solitude
    I reminisce
        About my past
            And oh I wish
That when I was *lonely*
    I could have *forgotten*
        About
            Aches, pains
                And *all* I regretted.

CARE

LIFE IS LIKE A FLOWER.
   YOU WATER IT,
      YOU CULTIVATE IT,
         GIVE IT NOURISHMENT
            AND IT BLOSSOMS.
NEGLECT IT???
   WHEN IT BEGINS TO WITHER
      ALL THE CARE IN THE WORLD
         WOULD NOT BRING IT BACK
            TO ITS ORIGINAL BEAUTY.
LIFE IS LIKE A FLOWER
   AND SO IS LOVE.

TIMELESSNESS

Man proposes
   But GOD disposes
      The best made plans can go astray.
Now suppose
   They are roses
      They're just *LEAVES CURRENTS SWEEP AWAY.*

Communication

We've *looked* but failed to *see*
Reached out and *touched* but failed to *feel*
Nibbled and *drank* and failed to *taste*
Sniffed a lot but failed to *smell*
We've *listened* to it all but failed to *hear*

      All because we have chosen not to
See, feel, taste, smell and hear

LOVE

We deny it instead
> **Allowing each other**
To dissect one another
> ***Admitting* love**
For only *portions*
> **Of each other.**

GET TO KNOW ME

I possess natural feelings to love you!!!
> Why? I don't know. All I know is that
> it pains me when we're apart.
It also pains me twice as much when
> we're together and I look back at you
> and I act as though I am a
> perfect stranger.
> And I *am*.
> For you *don't* know me.
Not at all. Get to know me. Do so soon.
Our relationship depends on you doing so.
> E ach year we've been together you've
> failed to recognize the
> REAL ME.

YEARNING

The moon has brilliance
   About it
      It's shining so brightly
         So cold—slightly
            Alone—lightly
But capable—likely
   To be able to shine
In the warmth of the sun
         Warmly
            Softly
               Wistfully
                  Hopefully

TIME

MUSIC is universal
   It can be understood and enjoyed by all
The same as
   GOD, love, beauty, peace, serenity and togetherness.
Why does man
   CHOOSE TO TAMPER
      With what's universal?
GOD in his infinite wisdom made "Time" universal also.
   However, there is *one* time man
            Cannot tamper with.

AWARENESS

And I've passed this way before
    It's just that now   I've stopped
To rest-relax-experience and enjoy
    The Beauty of "GOD"
    The splendor in the grass
    The softness of rain
    Aroma of a flower
    The sound of running water
    The beauty of love
    The gentleness of the breeze
    The sweetness of "Life"

PREVENTION

I wanted to love you, be with you
    Share my time with you
        Laughing, smiling, holding hands
           Running, collapsing beneath the tree
I wanted to place your head upon my lap
    Have our eyes lock—lips meet
        And we kiss a deep sweet stirring kiss
Our lips searching hungrily for the answers
    What's preventing us from being together?
     Why do we stay apart?
    What's causing us to keep our distance?
     Why are we breaking our hearts?

PAST, PRESENT, FUTURE

Yesterday, I cried a tear
   Today, I do not fear
      My tomorrow without you dear
         Cause I've been lonely over a year
Mostly because I can't find a man
   Who would understand
      I can't be his at his command
         Whenever he holds my hand
He should try to respect me
   And all I want to be
      And if he is too blind to see
         Then he'll have to set me free
I can't settle for being a part time love
   Being available only when he think of
      Soaring me to the height above
         Flying high like two love doves
I need someone to come my way
   Someone with me any night any day
      Someone who won't leave me when I say stay
         When I'm down and out make me feel gay.

A VICIOUS CYCLE

I don't know me and the reason why is because I am afraid.
I am afraid because I don't like the things I do.
The things I do causes me to be afraid.
Afraid because I must admit that I am wrong.
I am wrong only because I won't admit.
The things I do are wrong and I am afraid.
That if I admit the things I do are wrong.
I would hate me instead of what I am doing wrong.
I'm doing wrong because I am afraid I don't know me.
I don't know me and the reason why is because I am afraid.

MY LIGHT WITHIN

In the *midst* of a storm
    I have found
        A *ray* of sunlight
           Within me
I will cry no more
    I will be strong
        The tears have left
           No room for fear
The ray of sunlight
    Will grow brighter
        As I allow
           My burdens to lighten
In the *midst* of a storm
    I have found
        Within me glows
          The *SON.*

I AM

I am passion, joy and ecstasy—all the reasons for staying alive
I am a ray of sunshine in a storm—I shine constantly from 9 to 5
I am a rose without the thorns—beautiful, delicate and torn to shreds
I am the mist within your eyes—it's better than being your tears instead.
For as the mist—I am your conscious—and I will always be your guide
For tears are expressions of emotions which you can't lie, deny or hide
I'm full of hopes, dreams and desires—I've got to be strong and live
This life as I was meant to—for I have lots of love to give.

THE CIRCLE

There is a big difference
   In loving someone
      And in being in love.
I have to learn
   To know that difference.
      No, I have to acknowledge
I know the difference
   For I am surrounded by love.

WHAT LOVE SHOUL D BE

A feeling of oneness   a feeling of joy
A feeling of warmth   forever more
A feeling of togetherness   one of caring
A feeling of security   one of sharing
A feeling of closeness   a feeling of trust
A feeling of belonging   is certainly a must
A feeling of tenderness   and sincerity
This to me   is what love should be.

8/11/88

IS IT POSSIBLE
   THAT WHAT WE THINK OF
      AS OUR LIFE
         IS A DREAM
AND OUR DREAMS
   ARE ACTUALLY A REALITY?
IF SO, MY REALITY IS A NIGHTMARE!!!

VIRTUES

I have time on my side
I have patience to be my guide
I have thoughts to let me see
That one day I'll live happily

In my heart I trust my man
This I hope he understand
I'll do him good the rest of my life
And try to be the dutiful wife

I'll be his strength when he's in need
Be wise, kind and open minded when I speak
I'll fix his meals regardless of time
I'll wash his body and let him wash mine

Do housework, chores and care for clothing
Washing, sewing, ironing, including folding
Help financial situations by earning income
And use some of the time to have some fun

I'll strive to do this because he is my love
Happiness for him is what I think of
But something is still missing from our life
For he told me he does not want a wife

But I have time on my side
And I have patience as my guide
I have strong faith within my heart
That the love we share will never part.

ANOTHER DAY

Another day—another evening—but somehow it was different
It was full of hopes—full of dreams—because I socialized with friends in it
One a woman—who is for real—another, a man who loves me still
One's a stranger who I like—he's intelligent—he's alright

I found myself—shutting up—'bout letting him know what I'm about
But he in turn didn't do the same—I found he did not shut me out
I did not share what I kept hidden—I don't trust him—I really don't dare
I feel relaxed—but I feel I know—they're the only feelings I will bare.

I ACHE

I ache in thought—not in deeds—though people think I do
But I ache with desires—to fulfill needs—and know that they do to
They ache with desire—to make love to me—and I just play the game
Of letting them think—one day they will—for that is their aim
I ache in thought—not in deeds—though people say other wise
But I ache with desire—to one day show—that all they told were lies.

BELIEVE

Believe has a lie directly in the middle
Be evil is also contained in the riddle
Live-evil the letters are the same
Read them left or right you still suffer pain

I have a tendency of believing a lie
I have the capability to hide or deny
"truth" when someone really hurts me
If can cause me to *be evil* you see

I want to drop this word from my life
I think it's the cause of me suffering strife
To deal with throughout my past 4000 days
While dealing with people and their ways

Phyllis Ames-Bey

PURE LOVE

Love is not only a feeling—it's words put into action
It goes through three stages—the first stage is attraction
If I find you interest me—I would go about my ways
In trying to get to have you—for the rest of my days

The second stage has caused—a lot of confusion
Cause one mistaken it for love—instead of an illusion
It can cause you to act—without hesitation
It will make you blind to everything—it's infatuation

The third stage is pure love—and it's shown in every way
And if it's true you don't need words to express it everyday
For it is being shown with every breath you take
And true actions and reactions show it's no mistake

So, love is not only a feeling—it's words put into action
The first stage is attraction—based on your reaction
The second, infatuation—and there's no hesitation
The third a true pure love—blessed—with no reservation

PEACE II

Peace within—my soul—I feel
Will help make my mind free
Peace—within my heart—I know
Has got to be the key

Peace within my soul—I think
Will one day always be
When I find truth within my soul
Cause it will set me free

Peace of mind is hard to find
This much I can admit
And that is why I always cry
When I experience it

I cry because—I think of
Its beauty-its calmness-ease
Knowing that it won't be long
Before the feeling cease.

LOVE

Being able to reveal my innermost being
And hoping his mind won't stop him from seeing
My deepest emotions—my wants—my needs
My innermost thought and feeling with ease
Being able to share my thoughts and hopes
Frustration and pain and helping me to cope
Sharing my joy—my happiness—and at least
Sharing a home with trust and honesty
But most of all I need love to live
I need to live and love and completely give
My innermost all with trust and honesty
In order to share my ecstasy.

I NEED SOMEONE

I need someone to turn to—who understands me
I need someone to turn to who'll supply my every need
I need someone beside me to cease my loneliness
I want to turn to that someone—to share happiness.

I need someone to be my strength when I feel I'm weak
I need someone to be my guide when I astray my feet
I need someone to talk to me when I seek assurance
I want to turn to that someone when I need romance.

I need someone to comfort me to stop feeling negative
I need someone to share my life—I have a lot to give
I need someone to hold me tight and make me feel secure
Someone to share my ups and downs and whatever else I endure.

INTENSE AFFECTION

What is something which is often shared
What is never uncertain and always there
What is something that never need lies
The answer is love—and it never dies
    It becomes stronger as it grow
    It consumes your life with a glow
    It becomes stronger when things are rough
    It lasts longer when the going is tough
If you love someone and it is not an affair
Don't say "I don't love you" if you really care
Cause emotional love is not the case
But physical love is—if it grew in haste
    If you break up and are all alone
    Thank God for life—when you get home
    Cause the physical love could not have last
    Since it wasn't true love—it left you fast
It left you feeling all alone
It left you waiting by the phone
It made you wonder about your future
If a reconciliation would be mutual
    But eventually, you'll find as you live each day
    Pain and memories soon pass away
    You'll also find you'll meet someone new
    And be able to recognize a love that's true
Whatever you experience—don't shut your heart to love
For it's one of the commandments from God above
For love is life and life is empty
If you shut your heart and settle for empathy

NEXT CASE

My days are not as dreary
    As they used to be
For I look forward to my night
    And how evenings will be
My nights are not as lonely
    As they use to be
For I now share-some of them with
    People who understand me
My life is not as empty
    As it used to be
For I've changed my way of thinking
    And let others get close to me.

LOVE

Where there is love—you notice the dew
    The flowers, trees and starlight too
You're treasuring moments—holding hands
    Tender times—sharing all you can
Laughing over—a silly joke
    Relaxing from—a gentle stroke
Happy times—with joy surging
    Going shopping—sometimes splurging
Where there is love—you notice the stream
    Of light from the sun—or even moonbeam
You notice it makes you—feel aglow
    And also makes you happy to know
Your love is pure—your love is sure
    It's true and will last—forever more.

24 HOURS

I awaken in the morning and prepare myself for work
Sometimes I don't want to go in-especially when I'm hurt
I hurt because I've just awaken—from unrest sleep
All because I have no one—to snuggle with for keeps
    I work all during the morning-till noon time rolls around
    I throw myself within my work-because I'm feeling down
    Mainly because I face the fact-that at five when I'm through
    I have nothing to look forward to-and nothing else to do
In the evening after work-I visit my favorite bar
I sit; drink, dance and socialize-cause home is not that far
At home there's no one but me-for my son is still down South
I don't feel up to cooking food for feeding just one mouth
    At night I go back home to sleep alone or with a friend
    For the sake of awakening wrapped in arms-I hope the night doesn't end
    For I'm tires of going through life feeling lonely and unloved
    Being alone and feeling blue or forgotten by God above.

WARMTH VERSES COLDNESS

Hot on the inside   cold to the touch
Caused mainly by   a burning desire
Of her being loved so very much
And only love can quench the raging fire

Hot on the inside   cold to the touch
Mainly because she avoids being hurt
By getting involved with love and such
And refusing to be treated as though she's dirt

Hot on the inside   cold to the touch
Afraid to show just how she feels
And in being afraid she suppresses much
But in being this way   she's being real.

GOODBYE

10:25pm my dear and I'm sitting here wishing
    That you were near
For me to hold you and squeeze you tight
    To love you passionately all through the night
Why do you do it? What is your excuse?
    Tell me before I feel oh-just what's the use
I really loved you I love you
    But I won't go on this way
I really love you and I've loved you everyday
    But love goodbye
For I just can't bear the pain
    Goodbye for I wont' let you drive me insane.

WHAT DO YOU DO

What do you do when you've got nobody?
Especially when you want to be in someone's arms
To be held, to be kissed, made love to and missed
And when you want to be thrilled by charms
What do you do then you've got nobody
To listen to your troubles and be your company
Would you do as I do? Go to the nearest bar?
Or sit home alone and fight the misery

CONFUSION

Men have said they love my mind
Until I confuse—them at times
They say they feel—disappointment
When they wish to feel content

But they should know and understand
I'm not dumb when they hold my hand
Especially if they feel they'll het a shot
And I know damn well—they are not

They tell me anything I want to hear
And do anything to keep me near
Knowing all the time—all they're interested in
Is getting next to my bear skin

And that is when I make them confused
For I don't intend on being used
To satisfy their hot desires
For I don't deal with no good liars

WHY?

Why should one have to be tested
Be exposed to situations again
To see if one learned from mistakes
To see if response is the same

Why must I be subjected
To constantly making decisions
In reoccurring painful experiences
Reoccurring aching visions

I've met someone who loves me
Now others come from my past
Saying that they love me too
And that this time it'll last

However, I don't want them
I refuse to take the chance
On losing the love I now receive
Just for an old romance.

MUSIC

Music always move me—it awakens my desires
And somehow it makes me feel—oh so inspired
It makes me want to express—what I can't put into words
It makes me also suggest things when I don't have the nerve
I love all types of music—it sometimes make me bold
It makes my body respond to it—it makes me feel so whole
It's there for me to write—it's there for me to sing
It's there for me to dance all night—or make love to when I fling

MY REASON FOR LIVING

This was a poem I choose to write while watching a movie tonight
    I was so inspired; I remembered two lines and tried to make them rhyme
One wonders about their *reason for living*, especially if they are constantly giving
    Everything that they possess their first, their last, their very best.
And in return they feel alone and sit and think and write at home
    Feeling empty—feeling blue—and in not having anything to do
They mope and cry and ask God why—life appears to past them by.
    I've been giving my life to everyone else and I've found it is killing me
There is not enough left of it for me, so I gave it up, you see.
    You know sitting alone with nothing to do-can make you watch TV
I watch the movies on the set—and then I study me.
    Jean Harlow, Marilyn Monroe—in stories that make you cry
In listening to the dialogue—I found out just why
    My life was—as it had been—but the reasons can't be told
I changed my life before the end—for sharing it meant more than gold.

COMPANIONS

REACHING OUT
DARRYL

I reached out for friendship
and found to my surprise,
my nights are not so lonely
and I look forward to sunrise.

For I found more than friendship,
I found trust and honesty.
Someone admired me for myself,
with respect and sincerity.

He appears to be a gentleman,
a person very positive.
He generates very good vibes,
and have no time for negatives.

He assures me he will love me,
forever and a day.
He showers me with affection,
in each and every way.

I will treasure him and that love
I will love and treasure him,
but most of all I thank GOD above
for answering my whim.

MY SONG OF SOLOMON TO YOU

"Set me as a seal upon your heart"
    This would ensure we'd never part.
"Set me as a seal upon your arm"
    To protect our love from any harm.
"For love my dear is as strong as death"
    But when life has ended, the love is left.
"And jealously is as strong as the grave"
    And envy is all our associates gave.
"The coals thereof are coals of fire"
    Love is what jealous people desire.
"And they do have a vehement flame"
    But so does our love, for that's our aim.
"Many waters cannot quench love"
    It's an everlasting flame from GOD above.
"Neither can the floods drown it"
    So ours will be forever lit.
If you would give me all of your love,
    We can defeat all they think of.
Darryl, let me share my life with you,
    Let us share everything we do.
Help me keep our love alive
    For it is strong and can survive.
So, set me as a seal upon your heart,
    This will ensure we'd never part.

"Song of Solomon 8:6-7"

WEATHER MASTERPIECE

I am the mist, at the break of dawn
    Lingering with you, all the day long
I am the breeze on a hot summer day
    Caressing and cooling you in every way.
I am the moon, lighting your path at night
    The star keeping you company shining bright.
The sun beaming brilliantly during the day,
    From dawn to dusk, with you I'll stay.
I am the heavy fog which clouds your mind,
    by causing misunderstanding some of the time.
I am the storm cloud when things go wrong
    But clearness will come when I am calm.
I am the ray of sunlight in the midst of the storm,
    Look within my heart for light and warmth.
I am the rainbow, but beware of my illusion,
    You may experience euphoria or even confusion.
I am the heat in the summer, cold in the winter,
    You feel the same in your heart now that I've entered.
I am the wetness of spring, dryness of autumn,
    Y our heart feels the same, when it ought to.
I am the rain which causes the flowers to grow,
    I am the aroma of the same when my breezes blow.
I am the honey to be gathered not only by the bees,
    I am the nectar to be savored by you with ease.
But don't allow me to be the essence in you life,
    because your happiness may depend on my peace or strife.
And I wouldn't want you to suffer pain or agony.
    While being your weather masterpiece, for you deserve ecstasy.

MY MASTERPIECE

You stand more than a head above me, love, I like your height
It reminds me of the clouds so high, morning, noon and night
And when I look upon you, dear, I hold my chin up high
For that is how I hold it when I look upon the sky

When I look upon your smiling face, I also realize
You not only hold me with your arms, but also with your eyes
Twinkling so mysteriously, like the stars above
Often making me wonder, can we really share our love

The moon is reflected in your smile when I look upon your lips
Soft, warm, moist and sensuous, how I long to take a sip
Of the sweetness I know held within to fulfill all my hunger
Let me share more of our kisses, dear, just a little longer

Your arms remind me of the sun when you hold me tight
You enfold me warm and tenderly, and I feel pure delight
Within my heart, a glow so bright, because we're a perfect fit
Within my head, a brilliant light, love is the reason for it

When I hold my head against your chest, love, I feel everything
Our heartbeats are pounding wild about what the future will bring
They're beating soft like an ocean breeze, gentle as a misty rain
They're beating hard and quick with passion, now steadily again

I wrap my arms about your waist and tug our hips together
I match my steps with leisurely strides, unmindful as to whether
You want the same that I'm looking for, to share a love with joy
One which is true, pure, freely given, and lasts forevermore.

MY YEAR WITH YOU

And you never even thought—that our love could be so sweet
And I wondered why it took so long—for us to finally meet
You took me in your loving arms—and love you held me tight
You hugged me long and tenderly—on our very first night
    It happened back in February—a few minutes before seven
    It happened on a Friday night—I felt I was in heaven
    You kissed me eyes-my nose-my lips—and I kissed yours—in turn
    You even kissed me on my hips—and the hunger within me churned
I wanted you so desperately—I needed you oh so much
My body shook tremendously—from you soft-warm touch
We sat-we talked-we touched all night—but we would not give in
We reached and held each other tight-for it wasn't the right time then
    But in May-we caste away—all our fears and woes
    And we decided if we'd just-be lovers-friends or foes
    For we made love all through the night—and we no longer cared
    We only wanted what was right—and that was what we shared
And during June you really showed—I was on your mind
You helped me out and we grew close—and shared additional time
July I cried for I gave in—to how you made me feel
I prayed to God to let us win—for our love was for real
    August—it hurt oh so much—for I tried to hide
    My need for you-your tender touch—and on you I relied
    To help my mom-decrease my stress-and even share my fears
    I must admit—I was impressed—and as I wipe my tears
I thought about me letting go-and sharing our lives as one
In September—I did so—it was good not being on the run
October—I loved oh so much—for we had several hours
To hold—to squeeze-to tenderly touch—and enjoy this love of ours
    November had its ups and downs—I missed you being here
    Since I don't have you lying around—I miss you not being near
    December is two weeks away—our year will just about end
    And I'll thank God for you've become—my lover and my friend

WHAT IS IT

What is it I see in you
Why do you make me want to do
Anything to make you feel pleased
And make you want to deal with me
        I see joy and I see peace
        But most of all I see that each
        And every day I spend with you
        Just—allows me to do
All I want in being myself
And knowing I'm not on a shelf
And feeling so free to share with you
Anything I want to do
        What is it you do for *me*
        You—allow me-to feel very free
        To enjoy life each and every day
        Doing whatever I feel-come what may
To come when I want to-go when I please
And just live life with so much ease
To be myself in all I do
In sharing that little time with you
        Just what do we have to share
        I think-anything—to show we care
        About living any day without any strife
        As we go about—sharing our life
What do I expect of you
Only that you let me do
All I want whenever I can
While accepting you as my man
        Just what will I give to you
        Freedom to do as you do
        And I will show you I really care
        In every moment that we share
How will it turn out to be
I don't know-I'll wait and see
I won't be a problem-this I know
Whenever we're on the go

How do we want to deal with this
Well when I think back and reminisce
I can only roll with the flow
For you will come and you will go
Just what is the bottom line?
Well I look forward to the time
That you're willing to share with me
And in me being—all I can be.

TIMES

There are times   when I feel   very lonely
There are times   when I   feel blue
There are times   I cry   "God send me someone"
Now's the time   he has sent me you

To hold me close   to fill my empty arms
To kiss the tears   and enjoy the warmth
Of sharing love   and sharing time
We'll do it all   with peace of mind

There were times   when I felt   very lonely
There were times   when I felt so blue
There were times   I used to cry so often
Now I don't   cause God sent me   you

DESTINY

What about destiny—what do you see in me
What do you want of me—what is it I can't see
You call me Sunshine—I call me Sunset
I have you on my mind—you have me so upset

I feel you don't know it—you can't hear my plea
But I do know you show it—and you know my need
You just see my silence—my face when I fret
I may not remember—but don't you forget

Ours is a beautiful love—that we both adore
And it's blessed by God above—it'll last forever more
No one can come between us—this-we both know
Our love is one that's full of trust-we love each other so.

THE BOTTOM LINE IS . . .

Since we've met-I've no regrets-cause you were who I needed
I feel I'm blessed-with happiness-cause our love has succeeded
I'll cry no more-like I did before-for you are by my side
For me to love-have-hold-and keep-and even be my guide
I'll call on you-when I need your strength-to share my time-the entire length
Cause though I'm strong-I'm also weak-and your strength is what I seek

When I'm in need-I seek a drug-I have it with you-and it's called love
I need your love-I need you near-and when you're not here-it's me I fear
All my reactions-all my cares-and all I've done—throughout the years
I need you now-love—it's no joke-with the load I carry-I feel I'll choke
I need your arms-I need your kiss-for you are who-I truly miss
I need your touch-your warm embrace-I need to see-your loving face

I need to feel your arms so tight-holding me all through the night
I need to see your smile so bright-letting me know everything is alright
I need to hear your voice so sweet-see your eyes twinkling when we greet
I need to smell you being close-assuring me you need me most
I need to hear your voice my dear-whether you're afar or near
I need to know I'll be with you-wherever you go-whatever you do

I need to feel your warm embrace-and your tender kisses upon my face
I need to see your eyes aglow-recognizing I need you so
I need to feel your warm embrace-for it builds our love on a strong base
I taste your kiss-I see your smile-and if it's needed-I'll walk a mile
To be with you-and share your life-with such pure love-and little strife
Cause I love you-please understand-you're all I need-*you*-my sweet man

Inspire me to be oh so true-in all I say and all that I do
I won't do wrong—I'll protect our love-you're who I need-who I think of
Just stick by me-be patient and true-stick by me-we won't be blue
For I'll give you—the love I need-and you will know-due to the seed
I planted when I first met you-cause I was lost-you knew that too
But now my dear-I have been found-I need you and your love around

To lift me when I feel I'm low-to be with me wherever I go
To guide my steps-to share my ways-to be with me my nights and days
To hold me tight when I'm alone-all through the night to keep me strong
To lift me up-to share my dreams-and for us always to be a team
So take my love-my heart-my all-take it all-this is my call
To you to take my all you see-darling-just let our love be

ABSENCE

Darryl, nothing's the same when you're not here
For I need you-not far-but near
To hold me in your loving arms
To thrill me with your enticing charm

To want me when the mood is right
To make love to me through the night
To touch me with a tender touch
And love me oh so very much

To be with me when chips are down
To have a night out on the town
To understand what's on my mind
To share with me some of your time

To listen just as well as talk
And sometimes even-go for a walk
To be my lover and my friend
To never let what we share end

I find I wait sitting near the phone
Hating so much of feeling alone
Wanting very much to hear your voice
But I know that it was my choice

To be yours instead of his
To accept our friendship as it is
But that's okay for I feel much joy
In being yours-maybe-forever more.

BETWEEN YOU AND ME

Darryl, let me make love to you
Let me tell you what I would do
I'll hold you in my loving arms
And thrill you dear with all my charms

I'll nibble on your little ear
And whisper that I love you dear
I'll let you look within my eyes
And hope-my love-you realize

Just how much I love you so
With hopes you'll never let me go
I'll kiss you on your tender lips
And press against you with my hips

I'll put my head against your chest
Next I would let you suck my breast

I'll open dear my legs real wide
And let you slide very deep inside
And then I'll wrap you oh so tight
And make sweet love all through the night

And just when you're about to come
I'll try to make us feel as one
While we're climbing to the highest height
I'll give you tender—sweet love bites

Then my love—I'll finally explode
While we are heatedly enfold
Then I'd start all over again
I'd start by softly calling your name.

LET 'S MAKE LOVE

Make love to me-I need you so
Let's take this time to just let go
All the feelings we feel within
As being a lover and a friend
    Let us start by me kissing your eyes
    For when I look in them I realize
    You anticipate all that I feel
    And I'll show you our love is real
Next let me kiss you on your lips
As you hold me about my hips
Then your chest-I'll rub tenderly
While you have your hand upon my knee
    Let me wrap you in my arms
    While you thrill me with your charms
    Let me set your soul on fire
    Let me show all I desire
Let me open my legs wide
While you slide deeply up inside
Let's make love and just explode
And let's just leave this poem untold.

LET ME

Hold me dear within your arms
Fill me dear with all your charms
Kiss me—set my soul afire
Fill me with a lot of desire
    Kiss me love upon my eyes
    Move to my lips and realize
    I'm full of love-full of desire
    My very being is set afire
Milk my breast and warm my hole
Let *me* speak feelings left untold
Let my knees squeeze you tight
As you fill me darling-with warm delight
    As I curl my toes upon the bed
    I want to change positions-rock you instead
    Let me kiss you upon your eyes
    And build the warmth between your thighs
Let me make you feel-how I feel
And darling know-the feeling is real
Let me rock your world all night
Let me hold you close and tight

I'LL UNDERSTAND

Reach out for me and hold me tight
When we disagree or have a fight
Look deep inside my heart-within
You'll find I hope we'll never end
    The experience we share between us two
    No matter whatever each of us do
    Causes us to make love by candlelight
    Sharing all-including love bites.
Set my being-my soul on fire
Fill me with all sorts of desire
And if you ever change your mind
About leaving me-my dear-behind
    Let me think you're still my man
    Until I finally understand
    That I have to let you go
    Help me dear-just let me know
There was no choice in parting dear
No matter how much I want you near
Just let me down very easy
I'll understand-this you will see.

UNTITLED

Whisper tender words of love-softly in my ear
Run your fingers gently-darling-through my head of hair
Lift me up with your arms-hold me oh so tight
Make love to me slowly dear-all throughout the night

Wake me in the morning dear-with a kiss upon my lips
Hold me oh so eagerly-around my arching hips
Plunge within me deeply-see my face aglow
Look sincerely in my eyes-and tell me if you know

That you are filling me with joy-beyond my wildest dream
And regardless of how we spend our time-we are a very good team
So-love me—oh my darling-with a love that's true
And I promise you-Darryl—that I will love you too.

FEELINGS

Now I'll *tell* you how I truthfully feel
I care deeply for you-and the feelings are real
And as these feelings deeply grow
I don't even care if you know

I'm beginning to love you-I've known it for a while
But I would not tell you—that's not my style
To mention it to you in any way
For I'd rather show you-each and every day

I want you to feel it in my touch
I want you to see it oh so much
I want you to hear it when it's unsaid
I want anticipation to go to your head

When you hear my voice—let it move you so
When you smell my cologne-even after you go
Let your thoughts linger—on what we've shared
When we made love and showed we cared

Even if all we do is just talk
With arms around each other-as we walk
Sharing all our cares in the world
While doing so—let's let love unfurl

LOVE ME

I love you darling-this I know
You should know it too-wherever you go
Take this love I feel inside
And never let me try to deny
    How I feel for you-so deep within
    Knowing I'll never let it end
    Because it brings me peace of mind
    For you are sweet and you are kind
Love me darling in return
Let our love forever burn
Reach down deep within your heart
To ensure we will never part
    Continue—darling—being my friend
    I promise it will never end
    Enjoy the pleasure and the joy
    Of us being together-forevermore

I LOVE YOU

I love you Darryl with all my heart
I pray that we will never part
The love we've shared brought so much joy
I want it to last forever more
    I think of me within your arms
    You thrilling me with all your charms
    The closeness-full of love and desire
    You setting my very soul on fire
I can't understand why I'm writing poems
I don't know whether I'm coming or going
All I know is-I want to be with you
Not caring what you say or do
    Keep loving me darling-right or wrong
    Love me darling all night long
    And I will show you everyway I can
    That I appreciate you as my man
Continue sharing your life with me
Continue bringing out the best that I can be
Let our love continue to grow
Let our love continue to flow.

CALL ON ME

Darryl, call on me when you're feeling down
Call on me when I'm not around
Call on me when you feel blue
Call-when you want me with you

I'll be your shelter in the storm
I'll protect you from all harm
I'll fill you with the love I feel
You'll have no doubt that it's for real

Come to me when you feel blue
For you should know what I would do
I'll take you in my loving arms
And calm you dear with all my charms

Seek me out when you feel bad
Seek me out when you feel sad
I'll share with you darling-happiness
And fill you life with sweet-sweet bliss

So call on me when you feel down
Come this way when you're home-bounded
Let me put your mind at ease
And fill your mind with only peace.

ROYALTY

I love you in such a desperate way
Until I look forward to just any day
That I can spend a little time with you
Just treasuring any little thing we do

You constantly-stay on my mind
And I thank God for any time
That we can share between us two
Quality time between me and you

I look forward to when we make love
And I thank God-the Lord above
For sending you-my dear-to me
And loving you for-you allow me to be

Phyllis-queen of all-that you see
With Darryl as king-on bended knee
Holding my hand within his own
And asking me to share the throne

I REALIZE

Darryl; I am thinking of you-wanting you here with me
Thinking of everything we do-and wanting the world to see
Just how much I love you so-and knowing you feels the same
Wondering if you really know-how I want to share your name

Life—has been—oh so good—since you've entered in
And I know that if you could-you would never let it end
Darryl—I have you on my mind-cause I love all we've shared
And I love the fact that you've been kind—and showed me that you care

Mere words could never express—how I feel about you
And I will treasure the happiness—I've felt in all we do
I'll pray you never let me go-and hope you understand
Just how much I love you so-and want you as my man.

OUR LOVE IS TO BE

Look at me-look in my eyes-and I'm sure you'll realize
My heart is full of love for you-in whatever we-care to do
Come to me—when you want me so—come to me-when on the go
My love—you can count on me—for our love is supposed to be

Darryl, wrap me in your loving arms-this will keep our love from any
harm
Have just a little faith in me—for our love is supposed to be
Love me-hold me-all night long—listen to my heart when it sing this song
Darling you send me to such extreme-until I can't stand it and want to
scream

Marry me darling-take me home—I promise you I will not roam
Rock me-thrill me-all night long—take all my love until break of dawn
Be with me for all me life-take me darling-as your wife
I promise I'll be true to you—in everything I say or do.

FINALLY

I realize what I have to do
While sitting-writing poems to you
I must find time to write my book
And let everyone take a look
  At just what I have on my mind
  When I'm not sitting—wasting time
  And they'll relate to what I say
  And wish they could say it anyway
Well dear I make this promise to you
Writing my book is the next thing I'll do
And readers will appreciate
And think that it was worth the wait

UNTITLED

I think of you each and every night
And all I want to do is hold you tight
I look forward to all the time we share
And find I hope you really care

About things I do with or without you
Of things I hope we'll experience too
And Darryl I want you to really know
Just how much I love you so

I want you-to be-with me
I want you to really see
We are more than simple friends
And you'll find out in the end

The two of us is a striking pair
Another thing—we just don't care
About who really accept us two
In all we share—in whatever we do.

MY LOVE FOR YOU

My love for you is so sincere
    I wonder if you feel
It reaching out when you aren't here
    Don't doubt this love—it's real
My love for you is oh so strong
    I wonder if you know
It'll be with you all day long
    Wherever you may go
My love for you is yours only
    To use as you see fit
My love for you will always be
    If you take care of it

I DESIRE YOU

In the midst of a raging storm
    Or the heat of a Forrest fire
Or even the depth of a deep blue sea
    You'll fine that I desire

You dear and the love we share
    You, your tender touch
You showing me you love me
    And knowing I love you just as much

I lay upon my bed and write
    Of how I love you so
I sit and wonder if we're right
    And need oh honey, to show

The love I feel, to you I give
    From my very soul
Accept it dear and treasure it
    For that's what make us whole

So I say to you my darling
    Let the beauty flow within
Take this love I'm giving back to you
    For it's the same you've drowned me in

Let the joy I feel within my heart
    Show you that we should be
Just promise we'll never part
    As you share your love with me

I PROMISE

I promise to love you   so tenderly
I promise to love you   just as deeply
I promise to love you   with so much desire
Cause my love for you   is like a raging fire

    I promise to squeeze you   when you hold me tight
    I promise to please you   making love each night
    I promise to kiss you   when you look into my eyes
    Cause my love is for you   I hope this you realize

To receive my love   I ask this of you
Honey love me only   whatever you do
Dearest show me that love   each night and day
And express that love   in every way

    I promise to love you   with a love so blind
    If you're with me   some of the time
    My love will be sweet   and it will be true
    As long as I receive   the same from you

UNTITLED

Why do I have you on my mind
Why do I think of you all the time
Why do I always want you around
Whether feeling up and even down

It's because you make me smile
And even want to walk a mile
Because I know I'll be with you
Knowing you want to be with me too

Let's count our blessings as they grow
Enjoy the feelings as they flow
But most of all let's just respect
All that we've shared when we reflect.

UNTITLED

Can you accept me as I am
When lights are bright or even dim
Can you try to understand
Why I want you as my man

It's because I can be me
It's because I feel so free
To enjoy the time I am with you
To enjoy—everything-we do

I CAN DO ANYTHING

I can do anything I so desire
    Love, since you've set my heart afire
I can do what I choose this I know
    Love since you've shown me you love me so

I used to be so sad and felt so blue
    I was so lonely with nothing to do
You smiled at me and entered my heart
    And I have been happy from the start

And now I do anything and do it well
    Since you helped to lift me from a lonely shell
I can now laugh and also smile
    Since I have you with me for awhile

QUESTIONS

What is this hold you have on me
Why is it I don't want to break free
Why do I enjoy the times we share
Why do you show me that you care

Do you enjoy me as you girl
Do you want to be in my world
Do you love the way we make love
Am I sometimes all-that you think of

Is what we share supposed to be
Do you mind if the whole world see
Are you happy being my man
Have we done all that we can

To keep this love of ours alive
And not taking anyone's jive
In trying to keep us apart
Cause they've done this from the very start

Take a look deep down within
Can you forget the other men
That was once within my life
Causing me to feel turmoil and strife

ME??? A WIFE???

Kiss me—love me—hold me tight
Let us make love all through the night
Experiencing all we feel within
Never letting the feelings end
 Look at me within my eyes
 Look at me and realize
 That we share the best in life
 And we'll share more with me as your wife
I know you don't want to do this
But I'm thinking about what you'll miss
Us growing closer and closer together
Unmindful of the time and weather
 I love you darling—I love you so
 And that's what I always want you to know
 Just take the chance of being with me
 I promise you darling-you will be pleased.

OUR LOVE

I looked-love-within my soul
And I saw all that I behold
Seeing my life within your eyes
And I saw my dear-and realized
 We've shared a lot of ups and downs
 And we still have each other around
 Developing and experiencing love within
 And making sure it'll never end
Our love is warm-our love is deep
I feel our love is ours for keeps
Let us do all to protect our love
For it was given from God above
 The foundation of it is our friendship
 And understanding is in the mix
 Let's protect these feelings that we share
 Knowing-for each other-we'll always be there.

UNTITLED

Can I be the woman in your life
Can I be you lover and your wife
Can I be-your friend-in deed
When you need to turn to someone in need

I have virtues-count them one to four
When you come knocking at my door
Turn to me-my dear-my friend
I'm there for you-until the end

I'm there for you to love somebody
Turn to me love-not just anybody
I love you more than life itself
Don't sit and leave me on a shelf

Love me—love—and love me true
I'll do anything you want me to
Come to me when you want a friend
I'll be there with you until the end.

TEARS

And a tear rolled down my face
Cause I had no one to embrace
Feeling lonely and feeling blue
Cause I had nothing to do

I stare at your picture on the wall
Admitting I love you with my all
And more tears welled up in my eyes
Because—I finally realized

I'm settling for less than I should
And if I could leave you-dear—I would
For I deserve more out of life
For I deserve to be some man's wife

How much longer will this go on
Having sleepless nights-awake until dawn
Waiting-wanting the phone to ring
Wondering if this is just a fling

This can't go on much longer dear
I want you near-I want you here
If you can't give me a little more time
We can part-and I'll be fine.

DARRYL AND PHYLLIS

Darryl and Phyl per chance did meet—on a chilly night
Darryl said, "Phyl I love you dear and want to hold you tight."
Phyl looked up and said, "I know, I feel the same as you.
So hold me love, real close and long-squeeze and kiss me too."

Darryl held Phyl within his arms and gave a tender kiss.
Phyl broke down and started to cry and said, "You are who I've missed,
In my constant search for love, joy and happiness
You are the one I can't resist and as I reminisce

I want to love and hold you dear, I want you always near.
I want us both to always share the fact that we *both* care."
Darryl looked down within her eyes and tilted up her chin
He said, "Pecantan, I realize you hold a lot within.

Dry your eyes, just stop the tears. We have the rest of our life
to be together several years—and maybe as my wife."
Darryl and Phyl now share a love that is tender, kind and sweet.
It's really strong and it is deep so it will always keep.

THE REMEMBRANCE OF 8/11/83

Your eyes beheld me oh so long
My heart skipped a beat and sang a song
When you turned you head and looked my way
You want to know what? You made my day

Goose bumps formed all over my skin
My heart smiled a tugging smile within
It also fluttered and skipped a beat
When I walked pass you to get to my seat

My face didn't reflect how you made me feel
My heart began to wonder was it really real
In you making me feel like a teenage girl
My body trembled-my toes curled

I tried hard to look into your eyes
I stopped when I finally realized
That you had someone in your life
A girlfriend,-a lover-or even a wife.

UNTITLED

I CAN SEE CLEARLY NOW-I'VE BEEN A FOOL
THOUGHT I KNEW BETTER-I THOUGHT I WAS COOL
ALL MY NIGHTS ARE LONELY-ALL MY DAYS ARE BLUE
CAUSE I HAVE NOTHING AT ALL-WITHOUT YOU

I SEE CLEARLY NOW—I WAS TO BLAME
WISH I COULD TURN BACK TIME-SO I COULD CHANGE
I MISS YOUR TENDER LIPS-I MISS YOUR TENDER TOUCH
I MISS YOU DARLING-SO VERY MUCH.

WHEN I LOOK UPON YOUR FACE

I looked upon your smiling face
And I beheld it full of grace
I looked also within your eyes
And something made me realize

    I really want to know you better
    And look forward to us being together
    True-I feel your love-but as a friend
    And I'm hoping it will never end

I truly enjoyed feeling refreshed
I also enjoyed feeling blessed
In getting to know someone like you
And really desire you to know me too

    But very deep within my mind
    Something bothers me some of the time
    Within, I really want to shout
    And let what I feel within come out

For I desire to hold you tight
And squeeze you dear with all my might
But I'm afraid it cannot be
For I could not stand you rejecting me

    So I'll settle for being just a friend
    And hope the friendship never end
    When I look upon your face
    Full of love, peace, joy and grace

YOU TOUCHED ME

You touched my hand dear-by mistake
And that's what caused the ice to break
I wanted a hug-a kiss-a squeeze
So desperately-I almost said please

When you were about to drop me off
Tears in my throat caused me to cough
I felt so happy being with you
I cherish it, for the time was few

When you stated you enjoyed the day
I had to cast a glance your way
And when you walked me to the door
I had to admit—I wanted more

I wanted us to brush our lips
And feel your hands upon my hips
I wanted to feel your warm embrace
I wanted a kiss for me to taste

The sweetness of your mouth my dear
But I was instantly filled with fear
That you'd respond by pulling away
While all I wanted was for you to stay

I WISH

Just being close to you
    Causes me to feel so good
There are several things I want to do
    And wonder if I should
Such as-running my fingers through your hair
    Stroking the side of your face
Brushing down your eyebrows
    While giving a warm embrace
I find I want to kiss your eyes
    Y our nose, your lips, your mouth
I want to share myself with you
    Without any doubt
I wish I could let you know
    about the feelings I possess
I wonder if you would feel joy
    Peace, love and happiness
Or would you be ever so gentle
    In rejecting me
Would you tell me, "I'm sorry"
    Because it cannot be
I'm afraid to risk the chance-so-
    I'll keep the feelings to myself
I don't want to lose you
    Cause of me telling you how I felt.

I LOOK AT YOU AND WONDER

I look at you and wonder
    Why I have no one like you
Someone who would share my life
    Doing things we'd enjoy to do
I look at you and wonder
    What does God have in store
Will I meet another like you
    Would I be happy anymore
I look at you and wonder
    Why didn't I meet you first
Why do I hold my feelings in
    To the point of feeling I'll burst
I look at you and wonder-love
    If we could ever be
But the only thing-that I'll do now
    My dear-is waiting and see

CAN I MAKE THE MOVE

Can I make the move-my love-to show you how I feel
Can I make the move to let you know-that my love is real
Can I make the move to show-my heart's real desire
Is to be with you always-for you set my heart afire

I can't label this attraction which I'm feeling for you
I can't explain-why I feel-I want to share what you do
I can't tell you anything-but eventually-I must
For how else would you know that I want you and your love and trust

WHAT DO YOU WANT

What do you want of me my dear
Why do you want me so
Why do you want to have me near
    Your answers I need to know
To help me make up my mind
To help me feel secure
To help me when we share our time
    To help me be able to endure
This yearning for love-or a single kiss
The warmth of your embrace
The lingering smile from remembrance
    Of your touch upon my face
A touch so soft and tender-gentle and sincere
A touch reaching out—holding-asking me-to stay near
Reaching out and seeking-feelings I possess
    Asking me to share your life-with peace and happiness
What so you want of me-my dear-why do you want me so
For I feel as an illusion-because I come and go
We both must go on-keeping our space-individually
    And if we choose-to share the same-do so carefully

I LOVE YOU

The power of three little words
    Could ruin a dream come true
If you hold them inside-instead
    Of saying, "I love you."
My dear that's all you have to say
    Forget about your pride
Why not tell me how you feel
    Way down real deep inside
You lash at those who care for you
    Because they often show
Feelings of closeness-all the rest
    But deep inside you know
The only thing you have to do
    My dear, is just confess
The love you feel you have for me
    That love-you won't express

WHAT ARE YOU REACHING FOR

What are you reaching for-my dear
When you reach out to me
Are you reaching for that woman
That you made me out to be

That woman with a low esteem
Because she can't find love
That woman you wanted to learn to fight
For the love she thought of

What are you reaching for-my love
When you reach out for me
Or are you reaching for that image
That illusion I portray to be

One portraying happiness
Face always aglow
One rejecting loneliness
By being on the go

What are you reaching for—sweetheart
When you reach out for me
Or are you reaching out my love
And was I too blind to see

The love you're giving tenderly
Full of warmth and joy
The love I've searched for oh so long
And have forever more

SOMETIME I WONDER

Sometime I wonder if you really love me so
Sometime I wonder if you'd really let me go
Sometime I wonder if you feel the way I do
When I spend my time with or without you

Sometime I wonder why you let me in your life
Sometime I wonder if you're sorry about the strife
Sometime I wonder it you're as happy as I am
Will our future be brighter or will it be dim

I try to imagine me living without you
I wonder if I'm selfish to want my cake and eat it too
Sometime I wonder if you'll ever walk away
And leave me, honey, facing another lonely day

SPLIT

I want to laugh-joke and really smile
Cause I've had you for such a while
Laugh because I feel at ease
Laugh because you're such a tease
 Joke because we have lots to tell
 The biggest joke-me feeling-oh well
 It's a joke because in the end
 I know I'll end up as just a friend
Really smile-I mean smile a lot
Admitting that all I've really got
Is the friend I find in you
Cause we'll split up-that's what we'll do.

YOU WERE SENT MY WAY

The phone rang softly in my ear
The voice I heard was filled with care
I felt lightness in my heart
I felt the same right from the start
    The voice was smooth and thought of his touch
    Really moved me oh so much
    Thoughts about his tenderness
    Thoughts about me feeling bliss
I feel this man is so sincere
And really loves it when he's near
But still I find throughout the day
Me wondering why he was sent my way,

UNTITLED

I won't say how you make me feel-because you won't believe
Contentment actually exist-but you'd feel so relieved
If you express just how you feel-to those that you hold dear
You'd feel the same as I-my love-throughout the entire year

I LOOK FOR REASONS

I look for reasons not to love you
I look for reasons not to care
I look for reasons not to want you
But—somehow—you're always there

Whether I want you here or not
You let me know you are what I've got
I don't know what I'm looking for
But what we've shared—I've enjoyed a lot

You came to me and opened my eyes
You tried to make me realize
That there is nothing wrong with me
Nor do I need my false disguise

Baby—you made me feel so sure
That I'm entitled to so much more
Than what I'm getting out of life
So I'll reach out from the depths of my core

To find someone who will understand
To find someone who will hold my hand
To find someone who I can love
Who'll love me desperately-if he can.

PEOPLE JUST DON'T UNDERSTAND

People just don't understand
What we are about
They don't want you to be my man
And want us to fuss and shout

People just don't understand
That we don't have any doubt
About us succeeding cause we can
And they are waiting it out

But while they are waiting-they will try
To destroy this love we share
And while they're waiting-they will soon realize
They can't because we care

About our love, warmth, tenderness
Peace, joy and all the rest
And also God has really blessed
Our love to pass any test

People just don't understand
But they will in a little while
When we walk together hand in hand
Down our wedding aisle.

BECAUSE I CARED

No I didn't go anywhere because I did not want to
I stayed home cause I wanted to share my time with only you
I watched the clock, I hoped, I prayed you would hurry by
If you don't come the night of this day I will not ask you why

I can not hide, lie, nor deny these feelings I possess
Because I know within you lay true love and happiness
I want your love, I want your kiss I want all you will give
But let me love you, share the bliss and this time I'll forgive

Let us both show one another just how much we care
Let us both really show each other with all the time we share
Yes you were really lucky I didn't go anywhere
For there is someone to spend time with but I stayed at home cause I care

CAUGHT UP

Damn—it's cold
    To know without being told
That people take advantage of you
    And try to destroy your soul
The coldness that I feel
    Causes me to appeal
To God above to tell me why
    The pain should be so real
The coldness spread within me
    Cause I'm listening to a friend
Saying nothing but saying much
    But still won't let me in
His mind-his arms-his empty heart
    I should have known from the start
That it would be just a matter of time
    Before he would want to part.

UNTITLED

I am trying to understand-why he holds his feelings in
Why does he put his head in his hand-and makes me feel I've sinned
What exactly is on his mind-why is he shutting me out
What's causing the fear I feel this time-he hasn't fussed or shout

Do I fear he'll leave me-do I fear his words
Do I fear mental cruelty-or not knowing the worst
I've done nothing wrong-maybe it's time I should
To deserve the feelings he project-yes-maybe next time I would

I DON 'T WANT

You may not know what you want in your life
    But know what you don't want
A friend gave me that advice today
    So I could stop my hunt
Of looking for the perfect love
    Because I'm hurting myself
I'm punishing me for being without
    And feeling like an empty shell
I know I don't want to be lonely
    I don't want to sleep alone
I don't want to lie in different arms
    I don't wish to be from home
I don't want to keep on drinking
    Nor continue spoiling my child
I don't want make-believe friends in life
    And I don't want you for a while

THE ROAD

The road was long and lonely
    And it was treacherous too
But I found out I had to travel
    It-dear without you
Though you traveled by my side
    I felt I was alone
You didn't hear me when I cried
    You didn't hear my moans
You saw my tears and thought it weak
    Of me to cry from pain
I pasted a smile upon my face
    You thought I was strong again
You saw my indecisiveness
    You saw me filled with shame
You even thought I was too strong
    And needed no one again
Well my dear-this time you're right
    I need to be alone
For you can't feel my feelings of
    Me needing you at home.

DELAYED INDIGNATION

Lightheartedness is really fine
I feel this way because you're mine
But I also don't give a shit
Cause I feel you don't want a bit
    Of all this love I have for you
    No matter what I try to do
    And all I feel about the day
    Is you are sparing time my way
But I don't want it this I know
So please feel free to rise and go
Go to the wife you told me about
Go home where you can fuss and shout
    Just you keep on your merry way
    And leave me be—I'll be ok
It's just a shame men go through life
    Lying about not having a wife

UNTITLED

Awaken my darling-rise and walk with me
Let us go about the day and honey you'll see
All the beauty of this life through my loved filled eyes
Feel the joy of being loved and dear you'll realize
All that we've experienced before we finally met
Will only help the love we share with peace and no regrets
Listen to my music-listen to my silent notes
Notes which only you can hear-so here is your housecoat
Come out of bed my darling-rise and come my way
There's a lot for you to see-hurry honey-to share my day."

SEPERATION

Ok—you win-I won't try anymore
To get you to come back through the door
I'll deal with my pain and agony
Never try to be a man's ecstasy

I loved you more than I could ever show
I loved you deeper than you would ever know
But I know now you meant what you said
Cause you went about your business instead

I won't cry anymore—I won't shed a tear
Nor will I contact you again this year
Cause I can see now we weren't meant to be
Especially since—I'm not yet free

I remembered you saying you were my man
But I wasn't your woman—now I understand
I know I must exist in a positive way
And accept the fact you had no intention to stay

UNTITLED

From 128 to 113-a lot of lost weight—in less than a week
All because I tempted fate-for love is what I dared to seek
I should have known right from the start-I'd end up with an aching heart
I'd be alone and I'd be blue-waiting for a call from you

And if by chance I saw your face-when we happened to be in the same place
You made me feel—I was a fool-in wanting you-but I'll be cool
I've sense enough to let you be-for you don't want bothering from me
Go on my dear-now I understand-you're nothing but a lady's man

I'M STIMULATED

I am stimulated—full of life
    No longer suffering—stress or strife
Because I choose—to go on my way
    In living each—and every day
I am stimulated—because I know
    You have me with you—wherever you go
Feeling free to live—as I please
    Feeling free to give—my love with ease
I am stimulated—cause you gave me hope
    Gave me love—gave me time
I am stimulated—I no longer mope
    You made me feel—gave me peace of mind
I am stimulated—to let you go
    Cause you thought—I would always be
Sitting around—loving you so
    But my dear—what you didn't see
I was stimulated—to analyze you
    Things you said—and things you did
And my dear—you really blew
    For I am all woman—not your kid.

I'M NOT THE ONE

I am not the one for you-this I must confess
And I don't know what I'm to do—to give you happiness
I once knew love and I was hurt-because I dared to try
To love someone-be treated as dirt-and then I'd sit and cry
Wanting only to hold my head snuggly against my chest
Wanting warmth and tenderness—peace and happiness
Wanting someone desperately-I thought you were the one
Now I see you're not-for our thing has come undone.

RADIANCE

The radiance glows upon my ace
From feeling the warmth of your embrace
My eyes are sparkling-cheeks aglow
And everyone in the whole world knows
    The joy-the warmth-within me race
    And the look they see upon my face
    Reflects the feelings within my heart
    And you knew that from the very start
The radiance glows within my heart
From knowing that we'd never part
When I look deep within your eyes
It's what I often realize
    Because your eyes reflect the joy
    And warmth expands forever more
    I know you feel way deep within
    The love we sought when we began.

IT'S BECAUSE

When I'm insistent about wanting you-it's mainly because I need you
And also because I'm feeling depressed-about being alone and feeling unrest
It's also because I'm feeling blue-about feeling lonely-trying to be true
It's because I need you love-you are all that I think of

LOOKS CAN BE DECEIVING

The face that one portray
    Does not necessarily mean
That what you see on the outside
    Is who they are within
There's been a many day
    When I just somehow seem
To look as you perceived me to be
    But still you failed to look within
I appear to be so many ways
    But just what does it mean
If I can be-to you-inside
    As I am-not as I've been

UNTITLED

Another night went by-without a word from you
But I did not sit and cry-for I had something to do
I read "My Book" and analyzed just what we're going through
I read of "Ruth" and realized that I would stick by you.

UNTITLED

A minor disagreement
    Will reveal an awful lot
Things we tend to overlook
    Things our mind will blot

But during a disagreement
    Things grow in magnitude
We end up being oh so blind
    And having nasty attitudes.

IF IT DOESN'T WORK WITH HER

If it doesn't work with her
    Would you please give me a chance
I would shower you with love
    And your life would be enhanced

For I would truly love you
    Like you've never been before
I would always be there for you
    It would be you that I adore

I think about you constantly
    And wish that you were free
I wonder what is on your mind
    Do you think of me

I know you wish to be my friend
    But I want so much more
For I want someone to run to
    When I open wide my door

THE ENCHANTED SWANS

A blooming heart surrounds them
While drifting on the pond
They're lovingly engrossed
Look at the two enchanted swans.
    Glancing at their beauty
    Reflected on the pond
    Beauty of the love they share
    As they glide beyond
The clouds which sail above their heads
The rocks beneath their feet
Their hearts reflecting radiance
The leaves floating to meet
    The lovers going on their way
    Together—yet apart
    Knowing love was there to stay
    For they shared one heart
We could learn a lesson
from the two enchanted swans
We could reflect our love like that
For we share a common bond.

THE GIFT S OF LOVE

Faith, hope and charity-were the gifts of love
That, my dear, you sent to me-delivered by three doves
A fourth one guides my steps your way-the fifth one aimed my head
To see your love, hear what you say and notice things you did

Little things to try to show—and have me to believe
That I'm to act just like I know—love is what I will receive
As the gift within the box—wrapped with tender care
Reflecting all the radiance—of true love to be shared

Roses bloom above my head—and trail my every step
And I'm timidly acknowledging—the promises you kept
In making sure our love grew strong—with pillars full of strength
To uphold what we want so long as it is long in length

With faith, hope and charity and given as a gift
Reflecting what is within our hearts and giving us a lift
And so my dear I ask that you to please accept from me
My gift of love that's really true that I am sending thee

Wrapped with expressions of my love and wrapped with TLC
Blessed by GOD who reigns above-accept this gift from me

THE ENCHANTED FAIRY

Long ago I used to dream
    About whom I would marry
All because she came to me
    My enchanted fairy
She said to me—have no regrets
    Kneel on your knees and pray
And when you do—just don't forget
    To thank God—come what may
For protecting fragile love
    As fragile as my wings
For you've been blessed by God above
    With happiness love brings
So reach out and try to touch
    The one that you call dear
And share with him all you possess
    Love-sweet-pure and clear

THE ENCHANTED GARDEN

Sitting among the crystals
On a mountain ledge
My eyes upon the angels
Dancing near the edge
    Sitting among the beauty
    Flowers growing beneath my chin
    The clouds pure white before me
    And I found out then
I'm like the nectar in the flowers
The crystal at my feet
The angels soaring high
And if per chance we meet
    I'll be the beauty in your life
    I'll share my love with you
    If possible, I'll be your wife
    And I promise to be true

HOOKED

I've often sat and wondered about what you saw in me
I sometimes sit-stare and wish that I'd see what you see
The beauty of a radiant love felt within your heart
Reflected glowingly on your face-it has been there from the start

    You say it is how I make you feel and also how I look
    But I fail to see me as you do because I've got you hooked
    Hooked on the love which we possess-hooked on the love we share
    Hooked on the joy-the peace-the bliss—hooked on our love with care

I may not see me as you do but I feel as you feel
I feel the beauty of our love and warmth of love that's real
Cause you've got me hooked on the love-we've shared so happily
You've got me hooked on that love-which we share naturally

MY HEART

My love for you is fragile
    It's like porcelain
I have experienced beauty-pain
    But love you just the same

I offer it with trembling hands
    And with a trembling heart
Knowing you will care for it
    You have dear from the start

Yes-it has its scratches
    And it has its cracks
And my heart has been broken
    By both lies and facts

But my dear I want to try
    Another chance at it
Just treat my heart with gentleness
    Or it will break into bits

QUESTIONS AGAIN

I think about you constantly
    Why won't-my mind just let me be
What are—these feelings I possess
    Which won't allow me to rest

What is it my heart desire
    Why do I feel this way
Why am I being pulled towards you
    And want to see you today

Would you innocently pick up this book
    And read the first few poems
Would you know they are written about you
    Would you want to flip some coins

Am I wrong in feeling this way
    Would you really let me know
Will you answer all the questions
    Should I let the feelings flow

THANKS BE TO GOD

Before we met I was alone
    Without anyone to call my own
No one to love no one to kiss
    No one to share my emptiness
When I met you I lost my heart
    I wanted you and a brand new start
To live my life as it was meant
    And to have you at any extent
We fell in love and as love grew
    I lost my loneliness and emptiness too
You took away my lonely nights
    And filled my days with sweet delights
You filled my soul with such desire
    My heart was hot with love's fire
You showered me with hugs and squeezes
    And tenderly fulfilled my needs
Your kisses set my eyes aglow
    And love for me continued to grow
And I thank God for sending you
    To share my life with love that's true

RELUCTANT

And the tears welled in my eyes
When I finally realized
That it was time for you to go
And as we shared goodbyes

I crumbled deep within my soul
My empty arms unfolded
For it was time to let you go
With feelings left untold

I wanted to ask you not to leave
And ask you to spend the eve
I wanted to hold and squeeze you tight
As love you as you pleased

And then I thought *the will* is done
For we both feel as one
And the feelings that we both possess
Is love and won't be undone

I'll let you go reluctantly
For you'll come back to me
And we'll pick up where we left off
And speak words soft and sweet

We'll love each other tenderly
For ours was meant to be
And I'll thank God continuously
For sending you to me.

I LOVE YOU DARLING

I love you so. My darling
Let me show you all the time
Of just how much I truly care
I'm very glad you're mine

Every since the day we met
You've set my heart aglow
Only you don't know dear
Just how much
Unless you love me—so

Will you let the feelings we possess
Increase as time goes by
And let them grow with happiness
Loyalty and pride

I really am afraid to hope
And I'm afraid to care
For my love for you is so sincere
Oh honey—let's just share

Each precious moment
With a smile
Now and forever more
Reaching out expressing love
Yet realize that joy

For us my dear just may not be
And all we may feel is pain
Continuously if others knew
The joy we feel again

So love, we must with both our hearts
Protect our beautiful life
Never let others cause us pain-
Mistrust or even strife.

LIGHT VS DARKNESS

I'm the ray of sunlight
   Shining ever so bright
      Your heart reflects the same my dear
         When we do what's right
I'm the brilliance of the star
   Twinkling at night
      Your eyes reflect the same my love
         When I hold you tight
But have you ever noticed
   When I'm not in your sight
      Something seems to be missing
         And the dark replaces the light
I find that I experience the same
   When we're far apart
      Darkness tries to replace the light
         Of love felt in my heart

UNTITLED

Tell me what you see in me
Why are you walking my path
Why won't you just let me be
Why make me smile and laugh
   Especially since I know I'll be
   Hurt again my dear
   Because I just refuse to see
   I will not let you near
To open up my troubled mind
Or get close to my heart
And though it took a little time
   I knew dear from the start
   I want you as a friend for sure
   But you should let me be
   For I may end up wanting more
   Than you're willing to give to me

LOVERS PRAYER

I write to you my darling-this my lover's prayer
With hopes it will inspire-you to really care
About me and the things I do-remaining by my side
To help me from your point of view-while trying to be my guide
    I write to you my dearest-of what is on my mind
    With hopes that you'll be nearest-me most of the time
    I'll tell you what's within me-with hopes that you'll be kind
    In trying to get me to see-which troubles to leave behind
I write to you my sweetheart-and ask you to forgive
The words I use in ignorance-as I express how I live
Sometimes I feel I'm just a ghost—of who I used to be
Sometimes I feel a lonely woman-is all that you can see
    I yearn for you my sugar-though the going is tough
    I foresee it getting better-it won't always be that rough
    If we should ever separate-it won't be done with ease
    For I wouldn't even hesitate-to grab you about your knees
To try to make you understand-I want your loyalty
To have you also share our love-in trust and honesty
So I write to you my darling-help my loneliness to cease
And honey what I'm writing of-understand it please

KEEP ME IN YOUR LIFE

Please honey-whatever you do-keep me in your life
As your lover-as your friend-and maybe as your wife
There is a need-burning deep-like a raging fire
I can't believe-that you have me-filled with such desire
    I do not really-wish to write-anymore silly poems
    What I really-wish to do-is—hold you in my arms
    I want time-to cultivate-these feelings I possess
    I want time-to share with you-just total happiness
The butterflies won't let me be-when I think of you
My stomach flutters constantly-I don't know what to do
Something pulls within me-it tugs my heart-my head
This tugging tugs so very deep-even between my legs
    My arms ache-to hold you tight-and never let you go
    My heart ache-to say the words-of how I love you so
    I cannot stand—when we're apart-for I feel lost-alone
    I just go out—to mingle-bowl-and wish we were at home
But even worst-when we're together-the words just won't come
For me to express how I truly feel-about you-my special one
Honey I want-desire-and truly need-the opportunity
To make the most of our relationship-so we can live happily

MY YEARNING

I cared for you for several months
But there was nothing I could do
I was going with another man
While yearning to be with you
There was nothing left between him and me
Nothing except friendship
But the words of saying it was over for us
Had to come from his lips

I danced all night but every time
I got upon the floor
I looked around and hoped for you
To come walking through the door
My mind was saying forget it girl
He won't be here tonight
I fought to hold the tears within
And your arrival made me feel alright

My eyes strayed while I was dancing
Then I looked into your eyes
Joy replaced the tears which welled
For then I realized
It was me you wanted to be with
I wanted to be in your arms
But I thought be careful girl
He'll dazzle you with his charms

The time went by so quickly
And I knew we had to part
Then I decided just this once
I'd listen to my heart
For we needed time together
And we had time to spare
We had the remainder of the evening
That we could actually share

REJECTION

I'm tired of experiencing forms of rejection
I'm tired of seeking any kind of affection
Because of the pain I feel from the two
I'm afraid of the moments I spend with you

I treasure the beauty of all we've shared
Somehow you make me feel you really care
Your absence and presence control my emotions
Whether you're with me or not I feel devotion

I can't stand you keeping me in suspense
But if I get hurt it'll be at my expense
Cause I'm letting my heart overrule my head
I'm taking a chance of believing I'm loved again

I'm tired of experiencing forms of rejection
And I know my heart needs total protection
But somehow with you I don't feel the need
So I'll be myself and let you proceed.

PERSERVERANCE

Today was just like any other day
    Until I thought of you
I thought about our moments shared
    And different things we do
I thought about you holding me
    And darling then felt blue
Because I did not have you here
    To hold me all night through
I thought about you telling me
    You want to see me too
But I can't help in feeling dear
    That time shared is too few
I'm trying hard to hang in there
    For what we share is new
I hope very much your love for me
    Is as deep as mine is for you
Again my love I want to say
    Today I just felt blue
It was just like any other day
    Until I thought of you

ENDURANCE

And we looked at each other
    Together yet separate
Neither of us knowing
    What's on the other's mind
And we turned towards each other
    Thinking of that date
With feelings tenderly flowing
    For it's just a matter of time
When we'll awaken reaching out
    For each other's touch
And realized we slept alone
    And miss each other much
My eyes will cloud my heart will ache
    My arms will be so empty
My head will bow my smile a fake
    Only I know I'm not happy
Yes we look at one another
    Not knowing what's on the mind
But knowing what's within our hearts
    Will endure all in time

TO THE ONE I LOVE

This is to the one I love
    Who shares his life with me
This is just to assure you
    That we will always be
Sharing our life together
    Including ups and downs
Cause I need you and hope you need me
    And want to keep this love we've found
The time we've shared has been very rough
    O n this we'll both agree
But I have faith it will get better
    Just you wait and see
Everything we've shared thus far
    We did not share in vain
Let's both be patient, be each others strength
    Cause I'm sure that things will change
Honey I really love you
    and I need you by my side
But I feel this love destroying us
    because we're living a lie
The pain I feel is oh so deep,
    words just can't express
The hurt I feel you're feeling too,
    and all the strain and stress
I'm sorry you feel I don't express
    This love I have for you
But honey it's there, I promise you
    And it's strong and true
And also love, your happiness
    Means a lot to me
But I feel you'll only be happy
    If I set you free
I'm sorry to say I can't let you go
    You mean so much to me

I know our life won't always be
    Full of misery
Somewhere down the line I know
    We will have the joy
It was there when we began
    And we'll experience it even more

THE VOICE -PRESENT TENSE

I hear a rich velvety voice with in my ear
Causing funny things to happen with my hair
A voice that caused my hair to rise and stand on end
When I think of you wishing you were near

I gazed deeply into sincere eyes
Eyes of understanding yes which realized
The hurt pain and suffering I'm going through
Gentle piercing eyes which sympathized

Your hands slightly caressed and filled me with passion
Very warm hands caused my body's reaction
Hands firm and gentle questioning and tender
Awakening my body making it yearn for action

I've dreamed your kisses were moist and tender
Kisses filled with urgency need desire
Sending a warm glow to the pit of my stomach
Causing me to tingle from my toes to my eyes

I want to experience your love making so full of love
Intense love making soaring me high above
A pure act of desire and pure ecstasy
The type I've always sat and dream of

THE VOICE -PAST TENSE

A voice caused my hair to rise and stand on end
It was rich and velvety in my ear
It was a funny thing which happened to my hair
Let me tell you what happened while he's lying here

I gazed deeply into very sincere eyes
Eyes of understanding eyes which recognizes
The hurt pain and suffering I held inside
Gentle piercing eyes which sympathized

His firm hands caressed and filled me with passion
Warm gentle hands awaiting my reaction
Questioning and tender promising satisfaction
Awakening my body making it yearn for action

I've had kisses which made me perspire
Which fulfilled the urgency need desire
Causing me to tingle from my toes to my eyes
Filling me with joy when I realized

I had experienced lovemaking so full of love
Intense lovemaking soaring me high above
The type I would always sit and dream of
So full of ecstasy until I screamed "enough"

FREEDOM

You carried me to the highest height
And I felt a warm delight
In sharing all I felt within
With you my lover and my friend

You held me close-you held me tight
You caressed me-all through the night
And I no longer felt alone
For I had you to call my own

And even if it's as a friend
I'll settle for that to the end
For I'm afraid to emotionally love
But if what we share is blessed above

Everything will fall in place
But if it doesn't we can face
Being friends both warm and true
And being sincere in all we do

Thank you love-for setting me free
For freedom means so much to me
And feeling free to be myself
Means more to me than any wealth

YOUR CHOICE

I will proceed
    Very cautiously
Cause I don't want
    You hurting me
Cause if it is really
    Meant to be
Things will work out
    Eventually
There is a
    Possibility
Of us being together
    Constantly
The choice is yours to make
    You see
But I know I'm tired
    Of being free

UNTITLED

No lies, no fraud, no bullshit
    Are the words you said to me
We're starting this relationship
    With truth-sincerity.
As associates-lovers-friends
    Or whatever we decide to be
We're starting the relationship
    With open honesty.

TAKE THE TIME

This is what is on my mind
    Seems we're always on the go
We should try to take the time
    To play within the snow
Take the time to try and enjoy
    The softness of its flakes
Don't think about how cold it is
    Watch the images it makes

DO I SATISFY YOU

Do I really satisfy   the urgency within
Are you telling me a lie   so I won't feel hurt again
Can you take this love which I possess   to be your very own
Can you take this love feel happiness   and make my house our home

Can I love you with my very all   love you day and night
Can I kiss your eyes your nose   your lips   and hold you dear real tight
Can I make love to all of you   from your head down to your toes
Can we make love can we feel free   to always have and hold . . . .

You close to me and me to you   and when all is said and done
You will be mine I will be yours   our love will be as one
Would you want to find me writing   when you open wide the door
Would you like to feel you have me   and my love forever more

So tell me do I satisfy you love   in each and every way
And can I count on you always   being here to stay
For I need you I love you dear   I want you for my own
To stay with me and build with me   our very happy home

BE A FRIEND FIRST

You gazed my dear within my eyes
    And I was glad to realize
That you're a man who is sensitive
    And that you have a lot to give
To someone who is somewhat like you
    Expressing same and sharing your view
About whatever come what may
    Life, love, friendship about the day
To do what makes you feel content
    And leave alone what isn't meant
Why our paths crossed, I do not know
    But I do know I'll take it slow
For if I don't I'll fall for you
    Because I know you're lonely too
I'll be open, I'll be direct
    And I'll certainly leave you if I suspect
A feeling that you want no one
    Cause you've been hurt too much by some
Person who did not take the time
    To know you, love, and know your mind
A person who was being unreal
    A person who could not keep still
Long enough to know you well
    But long enough for you to tell
She wasn't for you-but still you let
    She hurt you so-that-I regret
But I have hopes that you and i
    Will share our life by and by
Only start off by being my friend
    And you'll find out in the end
It'll help us with whatever we share
    It'll help us show how much we care
About whatever we choose to do
    When you see me and I see you

UNCERTAINTY

Evenings when the sun goes down
    and I don't have you around
        I feel so much misery
            and I feel so damn lonely
When I wonder where you are
    whether near or far
        tears well up within my eyes
            for I admit I realize
I care for you more than I should
    and wonder if we really could
        end up being more than friends
            following what we feel within
Evenings when the sun goes down
    and I don't have you around
        I cry because I feel so blue
            spending the evening without you.

SHOULD I FLICK THE SWITCH

Love is like a light bulb
    And when the bulb blows
        It won't light up—it will not shine
            Cause love is no longer mine
Love is like a light bulb
    And when the love is blown
        It was not right and I should have known
            That I'd end up alone
Love's got me hooked   Made me a crook
    Cause love has made me blind
        I was a fool   But you were kind
            Now you're on my mind

I STAND ACCUSED

I stand accused of stealing you
And that accusation is totally untrue
Even if it was-all's fair in love and war
Especially if you're who I yearn for
 I stand accused of loving you
 And that accusation is totally true
 You are who I wish to possess
 For my share of happiness
I stand accused of wanting you
To share all we can-between us two
Our ups and downs-laughter and tears
To be together for the rest of our years
 I stand accused of needing you
 To have-hold-and love me-whatever you do
 And in return I will bestow
 My love on you-untold

UNTITLED

Four days-no-four night ago
 You held me very tight
And we made love so fervently
 All throughout the night
You held me dear so passionately
 With warmth and tenderness
And filled my being with so much love
 And peace and joyous bliss
I spent the next day wondering
 Just how would it be
If we decided to spend our time
 Together endlessly
But then I thought-forget it
 For you don't even know
Just how you're affecting me
 Nor how I miss you so

LOOKING FORWARD

I cry within for I feel alone
　　And there is no way for you to phone
I cry because I have nothing to do
　　E specially since I'm not with you
When we next meet come into my arms
　　And then just thrill me with your charms
Smother me with deep affection
　　Look out for us with strong protection
Feel free to do the things you say
　　Know what awaits us is the day
Let us share a love so bright
　　A love that's sweet each day and night

UNTITLED

All around me I can hear-laughter-far and near
All around me I can see-smiles which seem sincere
All around me I can see the bustle of the day
I can also see myself-using time to work or play
　　Writing poems-poetry and songs so sweet-wishing you were here
　　Reminiscing about last night-and wishing you were near
　　To hold my hand and squeeze me tight-and set my heart aglow
　　To kiss my lips-my eyes-my ears-and make me need you so
This is such a different world-and I feel at ease
Thanks-for sharing it with me-for I feel very pleased
That you took time to let me know you-when you came my way
And dear I thank you very much-for loving me come what may

UNTITLED

The day is warm and gloomy
   The place nice and roomy
      And a soft misty rain
         Is falling against the pane
And I am so at peace
   In my solitude
      I feel relaxed and so at ease
         While lying next to you
The sunlight peeks through scattered clouds
   While I wonder aloud
      Whether the way I feel will last
         Or will it quickly pass

180 MILES

My feelings for you are sincere
   I wonder if you feel
      Them reaching out when you are near
         No doubt-they are very real
My feelings for you are so strong
   I wonder if you know
      They will be with you all day long
         Wherever you may go
My feelings are for you-you see
   But don't use as you see fit
      My feelings-love-will always be
         More than a little bit.

CONSIDERATION

Broken promises are not fair
    For they are signs that you don't care
About the things you say and do
    About the things making me feel blue

You told me you would pick me up
    I believed you dear-and I got stuck
Because you failed to come my way
    You knew you wouldn't come today

I will not wait on you again
    This way-I will avoid the pain
I feel when I do not see you
    Since you just care about what you do.

UNTITLED

Lying here beside you-I feel so at ease
Because you shared your love with me-you aimed to make me pleased
We belong together dear-and we should have no fear
As to whether or not it's meant to be or whether it'll last for years
I love you so my darling-I love you oh so much
I love the moments that we share-I love your tender touch
And darling as we live our life-on one thing let's agree
That we'll live it together in peace-love and harmony

OUR GROWN UP KIDS

What's the matter baby-why did I not see you
Tell me why you're staying away-why are you feeling blue
Why has so much time gone by-why have you not come home
Must I sit and must I cry-cause I feel all alone
    What is your excuse this time-is it something that I've done
    Am I pushing you away from me-or are you on the run
    Taking care of what you say-responsibilities
    Well honey-won't you make the time-to come and be with me

TRUE LOVE

Mere words can *not* describe-*explain-nor* express
The *beauty* felt-the beauty *shared*—not even the *happiness*
Of a true love *meant* to be-*blessed* by God above
A love withstanding *any* test-*any* man thinks of
I'm now experiencing such a love-deep within my heart
And what god has put asunder-*no* man can tear apart
But most of all everyone should know-that my love with you
Can *not* be separated-probably *tested*-but not used nor abused

UNTITLED

To you my love-I dedicate
    The feelings of true love
Treasure and accept it
    Let it be all you think of
There's nothing else I can bestow
    It's all that I can give
It's helping me not only exist
    It's helping me to live

I've seen the stars, sun
    moon and the earth
There's still to be seen
    the universe

IS IT BECAUSE

My love-you just can't help but see
    That as the seconds-the minutes-the hours past by
I sit here waiting patiently
    N ow I'm beginning to wonder why
Just why-tell me—why do I love you
    Tell me why I have blind faith in you
Why do I sit at home and wait
    Like there's nothing else for me to do
Is it because you feel for me
    And made me feel all you possess
Is it because I fail to see
    But feel you give me happiness
Is it because I see in you
    The man I so desire
Or am I fooling myself too
    Am I being just a liar
Is it because I want to hear
    You whispering words of love
And wanting you to soar me dear
    To the highest heights above
Is it because I want to smell
    Your odor in my arms
Is it because I want to thrill you
    With my tender charms
Is it because I want to taste
    Your mouth-your eyes-your lips
Or am I missing your embrace
    And your hands about my hips
The seconds-the minutes-the hours past by
    And I'm feeling so alone
I feel as though I want to cry
    For you're not here at home

CONSIDERATION VS COMMUNICATION

Why didn't you come by tonight
  Why didn't you come home
Did you go to watch the fight
  And leave me here alone
Why do you make promises
  Don't you know they hurt
Don't you know how bad it is
  To feel you have no worth
When one you love-can't be with you
  And makes you feel as though
One only wants you by their side
  When they need you so
It hurts because it makes you feel
  You're just plain old standby
And if that's all I am to you
  I am a fool and here's why
I should not sit and cry at home
  Because you did not come
I should say—girl-get up-go out
  And try to find your "hon"

REFLECTIONS

I think back on yesterday
    And the day before
And as I look back, I realize
    I love you more and more
I cannot picture going through life
    Without you by my side
And while I lay and visualize
    I see my arms stretched wide
To welcome you within them dear
    Each and every day
To hug and hold and squeeze you love
    With hopes you'll one day stay
I think back on yesterday
    And the day before
And wish that we would make up love
    For I feel so poor
For I don't have you by my side
    Do you think you're being fair
Do you want me to just sit and cry
    Or will you show you actually care

WHAT IS LOVE

Love, exactly what is it
Why does it cause me pain
I have experienced a little bit
And found I've searched in vain

I have a man I love so much
He sets me all aglow
I love his smile-his tender touch
And think it's time he know

About the pain he cause within
When he fails to come
About the pain he cause within
And don't know what it's from

It is from times I ache to hold
Him very close to me
I t is from times I've left untold
Of how he let me see

He doesn't always come to me
When he says he will
And makes me feel he'll let me be
And makes me often feel

Pain deep within my heart
Wanting him to hold
Making me regret our start
And leaving it untold

THINK

I sit and stare   why   I don't know
I don't even care   bout wanting you so
I feel no pain   no love   no joy
I feel no shame   about being your toy
I'm in control   don't fall for lines
Not saying I'm cold   just wasting time
But all in all   love is what I want
But I'm afraid to fall   I don't want to be taunt

No hurt   no pain no   cruelty
I won't allow it to happen to me
I've changed my rhythm   I've changed my flow
Cause I don't want you   to really know
That I'm sensitive   and I need love
That I want to live   and be thought of
I want to be held   and want to be missed
I want to be felt   and have you reminisce

All about   the feelings we share
And knowing that   I really care
Think about the night   I showed
I cared for you   think of the flow
Think of our hearts   beating as one
Think that our love   can't be undone
Think of our love   that we possess
Think it will bring   us happiness

MATURING GRACEFULLY

I'm sitting in a rocking chair
    With my mind on you
Thinking about all we've shared
    Though times we'd shared were few
I'm thinking of the day I left
    But what else could I do
I did so to bring out the best
    Of love in me and you
I've found I really love you
    I know I really care
I've found also you love me too
    Although you weren't fair
At times I felt so dog-gone-blue
    Because you were not near
I sat not knowing what to do
    I wondered did you care
On 1/28/89 at quarter after two
    I looked out the window
And watched you sitting there
    I wondered if your love was true
Did you really care
    I wondered if by leaving you
Whether I was being fair

METAMORPHOSIS

Once I was like a bird in flight
    Soaring above the highest cloud
        Because he was bestowing me
            With all the love that I'd allow

Once I was like a fish in water
    Drowning in a deep blue sea
        Because he was filling me with love
            And drowning me in ecstasy

Once I was like a mother hen
    Concerned and over protective
        Because he was as fragile as china
            I didn't want broken or taken

Once I was like a cuddly bear
    I was always in his arms
        Because he was my polar bear
            Wooing me with his charms

Once I was like a tiger insane
    When he grabbed me by my tail
        Cause he was my lion and he knew
            That he would never fail

To fill my womb with sweet delight
    And rock me through the night
        He blew my mind all during the day
            In every imaginable way

And now I'm becoming aware
    That everything has changed
        Because he like a caged bird
            Nothing is the same

And now I'm really wondering
   Why things changed drastically
      Because he is away for oh so long
         When he's apart from me

And now I'm wishing desperately
   Our love would be as before
      Because he's feeling so disgusted
         He can't take anymore

And now I am opening my eyes
   To seeing things as he does
      Because he's feeling the same as I
         He wants our love as it was

He'll have to stop very soon
   His lying, cheating and phone calls
      Because if he does not
         There's no relationship at all

He will have to realize
   That both of us must change
      And then he'll find as time goes by
         It was worth our aim

MY CRAVINGS

I don't desire a cigarette
I don't desire to feel regret
I don't desire a drink or two
But love I do desire you
    I don't desire to be alone
    I don't desire an empty home
    I don't desire to be so blue
    But honey I do desire you
I do desire your tender touch
To be with you so very much
I do desire your kiss-your squeeze
I do desire to be pleased
    I don't desire any strife
    I don't desire a lonely life
    I don't desire to be untrue
    Especially since you desire me too

UNTITLED

My heart is soaring like a bird
    In the sky above
Because I know it's me he needs
    Me he wants to love
My heart is fragile like a butterfly's wing
    Easy to be broken
Because at times he is unaware
    Of how harsh his words are spoken
But deep within my heart I know
    The joy of love is near
Because later on he'll let me know
    That to him I am so dear
We'll go make love, share ecstasy
    Joy and happiness
And wake up in each other's arms
    From last nights' lovely bliss

MEMORIES

I'm in a thoughtful mood
    In my solitude
I'm thinking of my past the present
    And future life with you
The past was full of hints
    Also experience
It's not too late to make use of it
    Let's use our common sense
We've had our ups and downs
    Also our smiles and frowns
Now let's work towards some happiness
    This final time around
You seem as though you love
    O h so desperately
But if you do why make me feel
    You wish I'd set you free
Our life we spend together
    Can be so much better
If we start being true to ourselves
    And also to each other

BECAUSE

Because of the love we share
Our blood now flow as one
Because of our togetherness
Our love can't be undone
    Because of our sweet moments
    We experience peace and joy
    Because of understanding
    We will experience much more
Because of us communicating
With one another
We shouldn't have the need
To talk with any other
    About problems we may have to face
    Situations to be shared
    Solutions thought of not is haste
    Because we really care
We will try to do what's right
So our love can't be undone
And it's because we both realize
Our blood now flows as one.

CONFLICT

This love I have within my heart is oh so deep and real
This love I have within my heart is tearing me apart
The one I am bestowing it on thinks it's no big deal
I should have know he would feel that way from the very start

He smothers me with all his love and try to make me be the best
In everything I try to do but I never get the chance
Just to relax and make him receive the love I have for him
And *if* I did he *still* wouldn't know, our meanings are different for romance

"A LOOK WITHIN MY TWIN"

When I look into your eyes
    I feel sorry for you
Because I know you don't realize
    your mate is being untrue
When I look upon your face,
    I long for you not know
Those secrets confided to me in haste
    when your mate was on the go
Somehow I feel you're just like me,
    you just can't help but know
It's just that you choose not to see
    because it'll hurt you so
When I look into your eyes,
    I feel sorry for you
Because I know you know
    that your mate is being untrue
It it's any comfort to you,
    I will be your friend
If I can be of comfort to you,
    I will until the end.

PART TIME LOVE

Why don't you listen to, "Here we go again"
    By the Isley Brothers
Especially when it ask, "what can you do
    when you have no *one* and no *other*"
also listen to, "Don't say goodnight
    when you know I gotta have your love"
Both songs express the way I feel
    Cause you're not with me enough
I see you when I go to bed
    You don't reach out to me
You say goodnight, turn your back instead
    And I feel pure agony
I see you at the breakfast table
    And when you take me to and from work
I wonder how much longer I'll be able
    To stay sane when you treat me like dirt
The little time we spend together
    We argue and you criticize
Any little thing I say or do
    I wonder if you realize
You don't desire, want or need me
    It's just that you would feel real bad
In knowing another would have me
    And you don't want them having who you had.

YOUR FANTASY

I am who you want
I am what you want
I am you cure when you are ill
When you're withdrawn and taut

I am who you need
I am what you need
I am your drink to quench your thirst
I am your cup of tea

I am who you desire
I am what you desire
Your fantasy reality
I am your burning fire

REJECTION

You don't kiss me like you use to
You don't hold me like you want to
You don't squeeze me like you wish to
You don't love me like you have to

I miss the kisses filled with desire
I miss the hugs I miss the fire
I miss the squeezes miss feeling inspired
I miss your love and I'm about tired

Of feeling like I'm in your way
Of feeling your hatred everyday
Of feeling that you wish I may
Just go somewhere else and stay

LONELINESS

I use to long for love
    Yearn for release
        Have a man around
            Whom I could please
But what I've learned
    Is that loneliness
        With a man around
            Still painfully exist

UNTITLED

We're lying here together
    Unmindful as to whether
One of us should make the move
    To get us in the groove
We're lying on our separate chairs
    Not knowing if we care
To join together have some fun
    And merge together as one

My LOVER

My lover loves me, he tells me he care
    And I feel so good when he is near
He eases my mind, eliminates my fear
    Of me having no one to share love this year
If you believe that, you'll believe anything
    He has seven other women and he's doing his thing
I'd rather be lonely than to take him back
    So love stay out of my life until you clean up your act

SPACE

Our space should be divided equally
    Into four parts with three overlapping
None should be dominant or submissive
    N or should there be any gapping
Space is time space is love
    Space is anything we think of
But one thing we just have to see
    Is our space should be divided equally

TONIGHT

Tonight your kisses stirred
    Something deep within my soul
They left me burning hot within
    And feeling like precious gold
Tonight your kisses revealed
    The story you left untold
They let me know I was the one
    You want to always have to hold

UNTITLED

If you find an intelligent woman
    And one who looks good too
Look beyond the attractiveness
    For there is inner beauty too
I have them both and hide one or two
    Because people fail to do
Exactly as they feel they should
    In dealing with me and you

SARCASM

To live is to love with your very all
    To be at his every beck or call
To love is to live beyond your dreams
    Enjoying all or so it seems

I DON 'T DESIRE YOU

He has some feelings—I have too
Yet I'll never say to him "I don't desire you"
Because I know that I'd be lying within my heart
But I will say I don't love him just so we would part

He wants his way and my way too
He wants to eat his cake as all men do
He wants variety and feels no guilt
Expects me to be nice when he hurts me to the hilt

It seems the only way I can exist
Is by going along with this program of his
Bear all the blame when things go wrong
Let him rock the boat and sing the same old song

But the thing is I'm beginning to feel
I can't take all the blame and feel like a heel
If he wants to run that's on him
He'll break up our home for my chances are slim

I'll take about all that I can bear
But in the long run I'll find if he care
About me, our love, if he'll try to understand
Take his share of the blame continue being my man

I'm beginning to feel the best thing to do
Is to free him from me and my life too
He's set in his ways and too old to change
It may be best to give up cause things will never be the same.

TRUTH

I am not being true to myself
I'm not living my life to the fullest extent
I am not fulfilling my deepest desires
I am not living my life as it was meant
    I have a dream of how my life should be
    The fantasy must become a reality
    The only thing stopping my dream from coming true
    Is I'm not being true to myself and neither are you to me
It seems I always search your eyes
For just a hint of what is to be
I long to find out what's in your mind
And for the beauty of the dream I see
    I'm not being true to myself
    For if I were I'd be happy
    It all depends on me making my choice
    To live with meaning or in agony

THE SLASH

I held my heart out in my hand
And gave it eagerly to my man
He slashed it cruel with a razor
For really he didn't understand
    The pain I felt had seared so deep
    And I could only walk and weep
    Because this man had failed to see
    That I gave him my heart to keep
He gave me back my heart to mend
He didn't want to see my face again
The hurt I felt was oh so deep
Cause things came suddenly to an end
    But as nights go by I get stronger
    I don't sit and cry any longer
    I have no heart to give again
    So my need for love won't be a hunger

WISHFUL THINKING

I thought of you today
I thought of you in everyway
I thought about me feeling blue
Cause honey, I miss you

    I thought of you today
    I thought of you in everyway
    I thought about you missing me
    And knew that could not be

"I WON 'T BE BACK"

Riding on the train
    I thought of you again
        And in my heart, you know I felt
            The pounding of the rain.

AND IT'S BECAUSE . . . .

I thought back once more
    About what you said before
        When you angrily turned your back
            And walked out the front door.

UNTITLED

Why is it you make me feel oh so perplexed
I don't know what's happening from this moment to the next
It was just about five minutes ago just before you called
I thought I wouldn't be seeing you tonight at all
Just why can't I deal with this anticipation
Why can't we get together and solve this situation
Should I leave you alone let you go on your way
You tell me "Butter Roll" you just have your say

CONVENIENCE

A convenience dear is what I am to you
This I can say   can you also too
I wait for your calls but they never come
You wait for me to fall but I'm having fun
In knowing you don't know—I know-what I do
And that I am only a convenience to you
Let me tell you bout this latest thing which I have done
I gave you your freedom while you were having fun

AVAILABLE

I was available whenever you wish
To share my time to share my bliss
We'd talk about time spent with you
Doing whatever you wanted to do
  I was your love   I was your joy
  I was your hope   I was your toy
  Whenever you wanted to be with me
  Whenever you wished for us to be
I was your girl   available
To share your world   I was capable
But since you're still cheating   I'll also say
I've left you darling   I left you today

ACCENT

Accent upon the feelings we share
  If my dear you really care
About our love and what we do
  About the time I spend with you
Accent upon the tears I shed
  Cause my heart ruled instead of my head
Accent upon me leaving you
  Or letting you feel free to hurt me too

WEDDING DAY BLUES

All she really wanted to do   was share
Happiness with others   who loved them and cared
But he made her feel   she was asking too much
That society and loved ones   didn't care for such

The people she wanted   amounted to seven
She wanted them to witness   her beginning of heaven
For want of these things   understanding and love
Her man, his name   spiritual guidance from above

Peace trust   and comfort too
And sharing their happiness   with just a few
She's beginning to wonder   if there's really such
A thing of asking   for too much

For want of them   she lost her glow
For in his own way   he let her know
He wanted to get it   over and done
And that getting married   was no fun

But what he really   failed to see
Is it was the first   and last marriage for me
I wanted him to see   my purest joy
That he bestowed on me   forevermore

But how can that be   if I must suppress
My deepest feelings   my very best
No matter what   I hope that he
Have satisfaction   sharing life with me

MY WEDDING DAY

For want of love, a man was found
To take away loneliness, to be around
For want of this man, a woman changed
Using all to get him, for he was her aim

Because of the change, he became perplexed
Always wondering what she'd do next
For want of understanding, the woman felt
She'd give in to his demanding and any thing else

Unmindful of the pain she felt within
She would let him hurt her again and again
Because of this hurt she sort of withdrew
Immunizing herself, making him feel blue

For want of trust and comfort too
She tried showing her love for him was true
For want of peace she tried to express
All the love for him that she possessed

She loved this man so very much
She thought she showed him with every touch
For want of his name she wanted to wed
She used her heart instead of her head

She wanted this man for the rest of her life
She wanted so desperately to be his wife
But this man as always had his way
on what was suppose to be their wedding day

She wasn't allowed to let their family attend
and in addition not none of their friends
The preacher didn't let her vow to say I do
The ring wouldn't fit and the date was wrong too.

SONGS:

Inspirational

I'M NOT ASHAME

I was lost-deep in sin-and caught up in the world
    And was ashame—of the shape-I was in
But I fell-to my knees-and cried, "God help-me please."
    For-I was tired-of the places-I had been
I would drink-day and night-when I *was* of the world.
    I would drink-to the point-where I'd fight.
I was ashame-of the way-I was living—each day
    To the point-where I gave up-on life
I would go-to the bar-when I got off from work
    And I'd smoke-in *any*one's car
Someone said, "Child. Wake up-for you're on-the-wrong-path.
    Don't you know-that you're going—too far?"
Well one day-I woke up-and I went to a church
    The first step-that I took-was so tough
Full of shame on my knees-I cried, "God-help me-please
    For the road that I'm traveling is rough."
Then a voice softly said, "Are you ashame to love me,
    and ashame—you don't know-how to pray?
Look deep down in your heart-if you want a new start
    and I promise-I'll show you—the way.
I will always-be there-full of 'Justus' and grace
    In all ways-I will show you-I care.
Are you ashame to love me-serve and praise-and be free?
    Come unto me-for your sins-I–did-bear."
And I cried, "Jesus-I'm not ashame—to love you.
    Lord-not ashame to serve and praise you
    God-I'm not ashame—to lift you up
    for when I called you-I know-that-you-came."

tune available

LOOK UP AND LIVE

Look up and live, keep your head up to the sky
Look up and live, do not ask the reason why
Listen to the words I say, don't let your feet lead you astray
Learn to use your lips to pray, learn to walk with God each day

Look up and live, be undefiled and walk in love
And to God give, praise for all that you think of
Speak of his testimonies, meditate in his precepts
Trust in his word and walk at liberty, unto his ways have respect

Do no iniquity and walk in his ways
Give thanks unto him-give your heart-felt praise
Seek him with your whole heart
Enjoy your brand new start
Delight yourself in his statues
You're now on the path and must choose

To look up and live, keep your head up to the sky
Look up and live, do not ask the reason why
Listen to the words I say, don't let your feet lead you astray
Learn to use your lips to pray; learn to walk with God each day

MY PRAYER

Lord Jesus-I acknowledge I've sinned
Lord Jesus-I am so sorry I've been
Oh so blind-now I see
God please forgive and pardon me
Please deliver me Father-while I'm down on—my knees

Lord Jesus-cleanse the thoughts of my heart
And please God-let me never depart
From you word-it's my joy
And I'll stand fast forevermore
For I can't—bear to go on-sinning-outside your door

Throughout my life
I've been taught to praise your name
Give thanks for all-and know that-you are not to blame
And when things go wrong-I glorify—your-name
Lord, I adore-worship-and thank you
And know my prayers are not in vain

Oh-I love you-honest I do
I'll always-walk with you too
And for once in my life-I will admit that I was wrong
And I come to you Father-singing my prayer in song
For once in my life—I will admit that—I was wrong
And I pray—You'll be with me—Lord when I walk along

tune available

I THANK GOD

I thank God, for the joy, that I feel
    When I'm praising his name
It makes me sing and shout and dance all about
    And know that I am not the same
Just take a good look at my face
    You'll see that God is whom I embrace
        And take a better look and you'll see
            It's Jesus I please

I thank God for love and grace
    He bestowed on me in every way
I thank Him also for making time
    To walk with me everyday
Just take a good look at my face
    You'll see that God is whom I embrace
        But take a better look and you'll see
            I glow from his grace

I thank God   for his mercy
    I thank God   for this spirit
I thank God for listening to my prayers
    There's never too much praise—so
        I'll praise and thank him for hours

So take a good look at my face
    You'll see my smile is not out of place
It's from the joy that I feel deep within
    From God's warm embrace

TAKE A GOOD LOOK

People talk—cause I go to the alter-to bear my heart to God above
Oh but they don't know-I-do not falter-in-praying for them with love
But take a good look at my eyes
It's a shame   that you don't   recognize
That the spirit of God is in me   so why act surprised

Oh since I've joined   there's been a lot of talk   of what I do and where
I've been
But God's word say-you may cast the first stone-if one among—you-don't sin
But take a good look at my face
You'll see that Jesus is whom I embrace
But take a better look and you'll see-I glow from his grace

Oh outwards   I may look flighty
But inwards   I'm praying nightly
Just the thought of God's will being done
On earth as in heaven-won't happen till we act as one
Take a good look at my face
You'll see that God is whom I embrace
And take a better look and you'll see
It's Jesus I'll please

WHERE I'VE BEEN

I've been searching, I've been searching, and I've been searching
for days and nights in every way-oh yea
And I found him-I said I found him-I found him
when my feet were going astray-oh yea-today
Well you know I looked high and low while I was always on the go
          and I found him-I said I found him

Well you know one day I started out to play some cards and realized
I wanted to go to church and pray   and be baptized
My Lord Jesus guided my steps and led me to this church
And when I found him he told me softly I could end my search

Cause he knew I've been searching-I've been searching
Over here and over there oh everywhere
And when he came into my soul you know my Jesus made me whole
          When I found him-when I found him

Well let me tell you some of the good things Jesus' done for me
He cleaned my heart, head, soul, body, spirit and set me free
He did it when I lost my pride and dropped down to my knees
I'm so glad that Jesus saved me and I'm glad that I believed because

I was searching, I was searching and I was searching
for days and days in every way—oh yea
and I found him-I said I found him   I found him
when my feet were going astray-oh yea
Well you know I looked high and low while I was always on the go
          and I found him-I said I found him

WHAT GOD WILL DO

One Sunday morn-I felt so alone
   I asked the Lord to come to me
When I fell to my knees—and cried-dear God please
   Hear my prayer please end this misery
I found that I realized
That I was surprised
That he was calling me

And people say—that my faith won't grow
But you can tell them—it's growing slow
Tell them I will stay in the church
For I've ended my search
And wait on God to answer my prayers

   And oooh He's calling me (calling me)
   From the very start
   For He's deep within my heart

JESUS-JESUS

Reverend G. will preach the word-to God's children today
He will preach it good and bold-so we won't want to stray
Preach the word Reverend, Reverend—preach to us today
Preach till we feel the Holy Ghost-preach the word to his host.

See God's children at the door-coming to honor Him
They will sing and they will shout and they will dance about
Singing to Jesus, Jesus-singing to him today
All of God's children at the door are going shout and shake the floor

Some of God's children stayed at home-lying sick in bed
Some won't let anybody know—that they are sick from head to toe
They should call Jesus, Jesus-for he will make them whole
Within their hearts, within their minds, their bodies and their souls

See God's children in the church loving the Lord God too
We will love him come what may—with righteousness and truth
Love the Lord Jesus, Jesus loving him all the time
Loving him with all our hearts and from him we'll never part.

Some of us are troubled so with problems we can't solve
We should kneel and we should pray and then we should decide
To call on Jesus, Jesus-we should call him today
He will answer prayers to him-if his children pray

See God's children in the pew-praising Jesus today
We will do his every will and with him we will stay
Praising Lord Jesus, Jesus with our hearts and our minds
Praising Lord Jesus all day long-singing to him in song

Reverend G. just preach the word—to God's children today
Preach it leaving naught untold so that none of us will stray
Preach the word Reverend, Reverend-preach to us today
Preach till we're filled with peace and joy and love forevermore.

ONLY FEAR THE LORD

Only fear the Lord—and serve him in truth-with all your heart
And do not forget to consider how great-the things he's done for you
For the Lord has blessed and kept you-from the very start
He made his face to shine upon you and was generous with you too

Just fear the Lord and serve him-in truth with all your heart
He is the Lord and there is no one else-there is no God besides him
He formed the light and created darkness
And he made peace-created all from the start
He made the earth—created man upon it
Stretched out the heavens very dark and dim

I fear the Lord, and will serve him in truth with all of my heart
I pray he'll save me and free me from the pain I feel within
Lord have mercy upon me, remove iniquities-light up the dark
Forgive me Father-lift me up and clean the blotter recording my sins

Cause I
Fear the Lord, just fear the Lord
I fear the Lord and will serve him in truth
With all of my heart, and all of my mind
All of my soul, that is my goal
So I say to you just Fear the Lord
Just fear the Lord and serve in truth
With all your heart

SONGS:

Ballads

THE OTHER SIDE OF ME

(Spoken)
After some men become committed they take their mates for granted
and leave them all alone. They go out to socialize with others,
leaving their loving mate at home. She gives him just enough rope for
him to hang himself and he's still not satisfied. He wants his cake and eat it
too and with her he just criticizes.

Some even meet girls who open wide their nose and keeps them constantly
     confused
And with those girls they think the grass is greener-and their mates become
     misused
They won't give up either the girl or their mate-they only want to have their way
And my man has become one of those men and should listen to what I'm
     about to say

(Sung)
Honey please   don't make me become,
Cold-blooded   cruel and calculating
That's the side of me   that I'm afraid of
I don't know   but it's capable of hating

It can hurt you   and destroy you
And feel   no regrets
It can make you   wish that you were dead
And curse the day   that we met

I have met   that side of me three times
And I'm frightened   of her powers
And if she ever   get in control
May God be with us   during that hour

So honey, please   stop what you're doing
Stop trying   to drive me insane
If you don't want me   say that we're through
Please don't make her   come out again
Please don't make her   come out again

Tune available

DISILLUSIONED BY LOVE

I have been disillusioned by love
I have been even misused cause of love
Oh just once in my life let it be the way I've dreamed
For I can't bear to go on being abused by love

I wear my heart on my sleeve
I've tried my damnest to please
And just once in my life can't I be greeted with a squeeze
Can't I sit snuggled tightly in your sweet arms at ease

Throughout my life love has caused me misery
Love has cause me pain caused me to live a fantasy
Now I choose to face reality
I'll be true to myself by admitting that
You're not true to me

I won't live in agony nor will I seek ecstasy
And this time in my life I won't seek love I'll let it be
I'll just live as I have been all alone but free
And this time in my life I won't seek love I'll let it be
I'll just live as I have been all alone but free.

tune available

YOU GIVE ME STRENGTH

When I gaze into your eyes
I don't think you realize
You give me strength to carry on
Just the little things you say
Helps me make it through the day
You give me strength from dusk to dawn

I watch the smile upon your face
Wish I could feel your warm embrace
But honey I know that'll never be
Wish you could brush your lips cross mine
And be with me some of the time
You make me wish our love could be

I wish you could take me in your arms
Whisper sweet nothings in my ear
Love me and thrill me all night long
And erase away my tears

I wish you'd squeeze me tenderly
Cause with you I feel at ease
You give me strength to carry on
And when I gaze into your eyes
I don't think you realize
You are my strength from dusk to dawn

Tune available

ALONE AGAIN

(alone again) it seems as though—I'm singing the same old song
(alone again) it seems as though—I was meant to live alone
(alone again) it seems as though—you want to walk away from me
It's as though it's the way it was meant to be

Alone again-living in misery
Alone again-giving my all you see
Hoping and praying for love
Cause it's you I think of
Oh must I find me someone else to love

Tell me why—must I always—be alone
And tell me why—you must always—be on the roam
And why-tell me why-I have to hurt this way
And why should I look forward to another day
Because I'll only be
Alone again-singing the same old song
Alone again-but this time-it won't-be for long
Alone again-darling-this time when you walk out the door
I may end up in another's arms for sure
I may end up in another's arms for sure

Tune available

IT HURTS TO KNOW

It hurts to know   that you don't know me
It hurts to know   that you're blind to all my needs
It hurts to know   but how can it be
If I were the one you aimed to please

I found the answers   to all my dear
I found out just about everything throughout the years
I knew where you were   when you were not here
It hurt so bad I sat and cried a pool of tears

You don't know when I ache to be held by you
When I need comfort you don't know what to do
But when some other woman calls you on the phone
You run right straight to her leaving me at home
                    All alone and aching

It hurts to know   that you don't desire me
Yet you claim   that it's me you want and need
It hurts to know   that you can't see
That your love is killing me so darling set me free
That your love is killing me so darling set me free

tune available

COME TO ME

Come to me-I need you-and your caress
Come to me-let's make love-I'll tell you how
Reach for me-brush your hand-across my breast
Run your tongue around my lips-and your lips across my brow

Come to me-slip your hand within my own
Come to me-let me tell-you what to do
Reach for me-let your fingers—freely roam
Flick your tongue across my neck-when I turn my back to you

Blow your hot breath in my ear
When you stop and nibble there
Wrap a curl and gently pull
When you play within my hair
Kiss my legs behind my knees
And also my inner thighs
Run your tongue straight up my back
Work your way back to my eyes

Oh, oh, oh, oh, oh, oh,
Come to me-nibble gently—on my breast
Come to me-let me make-sweet love to you
When we're done, I'll place my head-upon your chest
Then you can tell me how you want me-to express my-love for you.

tune available

I SIT AND WONDER

I sit here dear and wonder if the day will ever come
When you'll reach out and kiss me dear without me asking for
You, to brush your tender lips cross mine
Share with me some of your time
And crush me in your loving arms while you sip your wine

I sit here and I wonder why I'm alone and blue
You say to me "I love you dear and I can't live without you."
Yet this love for me which you possess can't wash away my loneliness
Won't you take me in your loving arms to feel your hot caress

Causing loneliness should be a crime-a serious offense charged first
degree
The sentence should be spending time—with the one you hurt-that's me
I'll have a lawyer plea my case-I'll have a judge rule it my way
I should feel your warm embrace instead of loneliness night and day

I sit here dear and wonder when the darkness roll around
Will you be here beside me-or will you be out on the town
Should I wait on you to satisfy—this hunger that I feel inside
Won't you take me in your loving arms and ease my hot desire

tune available

JUST LET ME BE

Just let me be   your woman   your lover   your friend
Just let me be your everything
Just let me be   your comfort and your ecstasy
Take everything to you I bring
Just let me share   my joy and happiness
In everything I say and do
Just let me share   my love with tenderness
Just let me share my life with you

Just let me feel   your hunger for me you possess
Just let me fill all your desires
Just let me feel   your kisses and your sweet caress
Just let me quench your raging fire
Just let me share   my joy and happiness
In everything I say and do
Just let me share   my love with tenderness
Just let me share my life with you

Just let me know   your wishes and your fantasy
Just let me know your every dream
I'll do my best   to make them a reality
We will succeed if we're a team
Just let me give   my all with tenderness
Just let me live my life with you
Just let me feel   the feelings you possess
Just let them be strong sweet and true

tune available

I'M CRYING

Honey I'm crying, over you baby
I'm also hoping, praying that maybe
Things will stop going wrong
Things will be alright
And I'll stop lying here,
All alone at night
Darling, just what should I do
To stop my crying, while I'm away from you

Baby I'm hurting, God how I'm aching
But one day, I'm going to stop, my heart from breaking
I've been so dog-gone blind, that I refused to see
I don't have to live in this old misery

And I'm tired of dying, a little each day
I'm tired of crying, and somehow, someway
I'm gonna stop this crying and get over you
For honey I'm tired of being alone
I'm tired of feeling blue.

Tune available

SMILE HAPPY

(Spoken)
This is for lovers—people everywhere
All types of couples-even those who don't care
Idle gossipers—and friends who interfere
Unhappy couples-with their loved ones being shared
It's about my smile-and the reason it's here
Listen carefully-maybe you'll get one there
(Sing)
See my smile-that's upon my face
It's a smile-nothing can erase
See this smile-it's within my heart
There it'll stay-cause we'll never part
My love-it's there for all to see
There it'll be-long as you're with me
So be my own-long as stars are above
Let this smile-my happy smile
Grow always-with our love
People see-my smile radiate
Love I feel-not one ounce of hate
Lovers please-try to understand
You can be—just like me and my man

One time-I was all alone
You entered my life and turned my house into a home
Before we met-there was no one around
And on my face I wore nothing but a frown
Since then not a tear have I cried
He said we'd make it only if we'd try
What he said turned out to be true
Now I smile happy cause I am no longer blue
See my smile—that's upon my face
It's a smile—nothing can erase
See this smile-it's within my heart
There it'll stay-cause we'll never part

(Spoken)
Hey boy-leave that man's woman alone
And you girl—don't try to break up their home
Woman love him-show him in any and every way
Don't listen to gossip-no matter what people say
And man remember all your eyes see ain't true
Trust in her-stop being so quick to accuse
And now you baby-my love forever more
Let me hear you come a knocking now at our front door

(Sing)
I hear your footsteps-I feel you're near
I hear you knocking-come right here
Take off your coat-you look beat
Take off your shoes-rest your tired feet
I'll adjust the lights, "Relax-feel at ease."
Put on soft music-let in some breeze
Here's a glass-your favorite drink
"Relax—be cool-try not to think
Let's eat dinner-wash dishes together
Feel my heartbeat-let's make love forever
Open the door-lie down on the bed
I'll now cry happily and let you smile instead

See my smile—that's upon my face
It's a smile—nothing can erase
See this smile-it's within my heart
There it'll stay-cause we'll never part

RAINING TEARDROPS

Raindrops beat against the pane
And remind me of my loneliness
I face the fact that once again
There's nothing left to do but rest
Sometimes I wonder if I'm sane
To want for love and sweet caress
To want relief from so much pain
To want from life only the best

Raindrops pound against my heart
Logic races through my mind
Telling me it's time to part
if peace is what I'm trying to find
I used to wonder from the start
If I'd be caught up in a bind
For I know deep within my heart
The woman he need, I'm not that kind

Raindrops hit against the door
Reminding me of how I feel
The hurt I feel will deepen more
The ache and pain is oh so real
I realize I've become a bore
But my mate has become a heel
And now I wonder what's in store
Should I turn my heart to steel

tune available

YOU'RE ALWAYS HERE

I've met that someone   he stays on my mind
I no longer feel lonely   cause he's with me all the time
Now that I've met him   everything that we share
Means so much more to me because he really care

And since he's kind I haven't shed a single tear
He holds, hugs and squeezes me with arms so sincere
And since he's kind I haven't shed a single tear
He talks with me, listens and pleases whether far or near

I know he loves me and he understand
I'll always have him to be my only man
I'll love him so deeply with a love so pure and raw
Cause he's made me so happy that I'll give him my all

Oh, and since he's so kind I haven't shed a tear
He holds, hugs and squeeze me with arms so tight, sincere
And since he's kind I haven't shed a single tear
He talks with me, listens and pleases whether far or near
                    And I don't wanna live without him

Honey, I like you   I really care
Always be with me   I'll show you I care
About the things you say and the things you do
And you'll always have me   to walk beside you

WE WILL SUCCEED

Love, don't you know I need you here with me
No matter what I'll always need
You for my own and to share our home
We will succeed cause our love was meant to be

Sometimes we try when we want something good
We do so dear cause we know we could
But there are other times when we change our mind
Cause things don't go like we feel they should

(Let's stay in love)
Let's stay in love as we share our life
(For God above)
For God above help us live without strife
For as long as we do
All our dreams will come true
We'll succeed in all we do
For as long as we do
All our dreams will come true
We'll succeed in all we do

MY SONG TO YOU

I miss you and everything about you
    All the warmth I felt within when I was with you
        I miss your warm and tender touch
            Honey I miss you oh so much
                I miss the tenderness we shared between us two

Uh huh baby I miss you and the kisses that we share
    And I miss running my fingers through your hair
        I miss your voice your face your squeeze
            Honey it's you I want to please
                I want to show you just how much I really care

What is this feeling deep within-is it love
    Why is it you I find myself thinking of
        D o you feel the same as I
            O r are you trying to say goodbye
                If so I'll put back on my shield and run from love

Forever but

I miss you and everything about you
    All the warmth I felt within when I was with you
        I miss your warm and tender touch
            Honey I miss you oh so much
            I miss the tenderness we shared between us two

BE THE ONE

Be the one why won't you be the one
Who comfort me when I'm in such pain
Be the one why won't you be the one
Who satisfy me when I yearn in vain

I am your mate why can't I lean on you
Why do you hate me when I'm weak
I am your mate what else am I to do
Is another pair of arms what I should seek

Be the one why won't you be the one
Who take away all my loneliness
Be the one why won't you be the one
Who'll share my life my love my all my happiness

Be the one why won't you be the one
Who hug and squeeze and kiss me tenderly
Be the one why won't you be the one
Who take me in his arms fulfill my needs

I am your mate why can't I lean on you
Why do you hate me when I'm weak
I am your mate what else am I to do
Is another pair of arms what I should seek

LONELY GIRL

I'm just a lonely girl-lonely and blue
Cause I have no one and nothing to do
My days are long and filled with stress
My nights are much longer because I can't rest

I'm just a lonely girl-filled with distrust
Cause most men I meet-are filled with lust
The lust for my body to use, have and hold
They even claim I'm such a beauty to behold

Though I talk to them-they fail to realize
I'm just a lonely girl-listening to lies
Of them wanting to do so much for me
Such as giving me the sun, stars, moon and a sea

Don't get me wrong I love arms to enfold me
I love also to hear words which console me
But I want this from one particular man
One of my own-not a one night-stand

Yes' I'm just a lonely girl-lonely and blue
Cause I have no one-and nothing to do
Life will be something cause I'll find someone
To share it with when my days are done.

TO BE

To be loved-kissed-caressed
To be filled with happiness
To be held-squeezed and told
To come into arms—which will enfold
  You ever so tightly
  Oh so delightly
  In arms so tender
  They make you surrender
   Your all
  But be careful-don't fall
   So deeply in love
  Till you're sure it's blessed
   By God above
To be trusted, to feel free
To be yourself, whoever that be
To look forward for moments to share
Knowing the feelings too much to bear
  Oh cause you'll miss
  That sensuous kiss
  Cause you weren't there
  And it's not fair
Why don't you keep him near
It's not worth the pain
To experience loneliness cause
You missed him again

I WAS MEANT TO BE LOVED

Why do I let us exist like this
    Is it because I'm crazy
Why do I settle for an occasional kiss
    Is it because you amaze me
Why do I let you do your own thing
    E very night including whole week ends
Why do I tense when the phone ring
    Was it her or was it a kin
Why do I let you argue with me
    It won't make the situation better
Why do I feel that you want to be free
    And that you don't want us together
Is it because I really do know
    Though it's deep within your heart
That you really don't want me to go
    You're hoping that we won't part
Well honey you will have to change your ways
    For I'll no longer settle for less
I was meant to be loved the rest of my days
    Love I receive brings out my best

THINGS WILL NEVER BE THE SAME

My back is against the wall-but I'm gonna still stand tall
　　And nobody's ever gonna hurt this girl again
I've decided to get on the ball-if necessary fight them all
　　Don't accept anymore-but still deal with my pain
I have loved and I have lost-I wouldn't fight at any cost
　　But I do know I can't allow myself to go insane

I really loved a man-but he didn't understand
　　For us to make it we had to have that trust
I reached out and held my hand-he made me feel he didn't give a damn
　　He couldn't see the love I needed was a must
I have loved and I have lost-I wouldn't fight at any cost
　　And I allowed our relationship to become a bust

Even when we were with each other-I still felt all alone
　　Because he did not know me nor did he care to phone
We really smiled and loved each other-during the time we spent together
　　He made me feel he would turn our house into a home

My back is against the wall-but I'm gonna still stand tall
　　And nobody's ever gonna hurt this girl again
I decided to get on the ball-if necessary fight them all
　　And not allow myself to go through no more pain
I have loved and I have lost-I wouldn't fight at any cost
　　Now I know that things will never be the same

tune available

CHERISH

Cherish all the moments shared
Cherish all the feelings bared
Cherish all when I show I care
Cherish me my love
Cherish all the honesty
Cherish all that we can be
Cherish all that I perceive
Cherish me my love
Cherish all that I bestow
Cherish all that's left untold
Cherish moments that I share
Cherish me my love
Cherish all that we express
Cherish all we share that's tested
Cherish me when I'm depressed
Cherish me my love

Tune available

I CLIMBED

I climbed to the highest mountain
And drowned in a sea of love
When I drank of the fountain
I reached too high above

For that little special pleasure
I felt that I would treasure
I thought that I would walk away
But it hit me hard that day

I ended up drowning in a sea of love
But it's blessed by God above
I drowned in a sea of love
When I reached too high above

I cried out late at night
And you were by my side
When I cried I held you tight
You let me know I could rely

On your strength which flowed within
When I did I felt the joy
You've shown me over again and again
Of having your love forever more

I climbed to the highest mountain
And drowned in a sea of love
When I drank of the fountain
I reached too high above

I DESIRE YOU

In the midst of a raging storm
    Or the heat of a Forrest fire
Or even the depth of a deep blue sea
    You'll fine that I desire
You dear and the love we share
    You, your tender touch
You showing me you love me
    And knowing I love you just as much
I lay upon my bed and write
    O f how I love you so
I sit and wonder if we're right
    And need oh honey, to show
The love I feel, to you I give
    From my very soul
Accept it dear and treasure it
    For that's what make us whole
So I say to you my darling
    Let the beauty flow within
Take this love I'm giving back to you
    For it's the same you've drowned me in
Let the joy I feel within my heart
    Show you that we should be
Just promise we'll never part
    As you share your love with me

ME, MY SCOTCH AND J

I've had a glass of scotch   and   I've smoked a jay
    But nothing kills the feeling   of me going on my way
To rid myself of loneliness   for no one really care
    I have no one to call my own   and who I do-I share
And as I sit and reminisce   I wonder am I wrong
    In wanting who I have in life   to make my house a home
Cause I need him   I want him oh so much
    I need him and I miss   his tender touch
I've gotten up and washed my face   and the time is 8:55
    I'll call a cab-get out of here-and try to feel alive
Where do you go at 12 degrees   what do you do to feel
    Should I drop down on my knees   and ask God make love real

Why won't you help me Lord   while I'm on my bended knees
Why won't you help me   send someone to fill my needs
Why won't you help me   send some one my way
Why won't you let him   come to me and stay

I've had a lot of scotch   and I've smoked me several jays
    But nothing kills the feeling   of me having lonely days
My nights will be the same I know   for no one really care
    I have no one to call my own   and who I have I share
But it's alright, when he does come my way
    I'll hold him tight and here he'll want to stay
I will turn this ship around and then I'll walk out the door
    Then I'll smile, remove my frown and never see him anymore
I will survive with or without his love
    I will survive   I pray to God above
To ease my pain help me live again
    Ease my pain   don't let me so insane

MY FEELINGS

Honey,   I ran into you tonight
And it hurts to know   I still feel
The feelings I felt within were right
And what we shared was actually real

Honey I know the feelings I possess
Has bought me joy   and has bought me pain
But I would have felt pure happiness
If only you'd feel the same

I miss your hugs   I miss your squeeze
I mish you darling   more than I wish
I miss the moments   shared with ease
I miss us sharing   happiness

Forgive me darling   for I've hurt us so
By denying all   I had to give
Forgive me darling   for I now know
I need you honey   back home to live

I AM STILL LONELY

I find life is funny
    Life can be so cruel
You're lonely if you have no one
    And lonely with him too
When you're together-arms entwined
    You're both anticipating
The two of you to come as one
    And wonder why you're waiting
When you're apart-your mind's adrift
    Absorbed with wild daydreams
Wondering if he thinks of you
    And holding back your screams
These are dreams of loneliness
    Deep within your soul
Screams of anguish-craving for release
    From loneliness treacherous hold
I have someone to share with me
    My life, my time, my love
But I'm still lonely and I foresee
    Many problems when I think of
Me holding deep within my soul
    My screams of loneliness
When all he know is all I feel
    Is total happiness

WHAT AM I DOING WRONG

Why do I feel so lonely
Why do I feel so sad
I feel as though I'm empty
Why do I feel this way
Is it because I have no one
For me to call my own
Is it because I have no one
Waiting for me at home

    Somebody tell me
    What am I doing wrong
    Why have I been looking
    For so very long
    Oh I ache so very deep
    And got a lot of love to give
    To someone, somewhere for keeps
    During the life I've left to live

I say why do I have to feel
So damn lonely
And why do I have to feel
So sad
I'm tired of feeling
That I'm empty
So someone please, please
Come my way

IT WON 'T HURT

I am weak but I am stronger
Due to the pain—I won't carry any longer
I am sure about myself
And won't be placed on any mans' shelf
I am sad, but I am happy
Cause I feel to be me
And I won't let-no one-anyone
Stop me before my work is done
    On changing me-to feel positive
    Changing me-getting rid of negatives
    Changing me-before it's too late
    Cause I'm the ruler—of my fate
I was a flower-fragile and torn
I was cut up—and even worn
But now I'm steel-there'll be no more tears
Cause I've rid myself of all my fears
I was weak-but now I'm stronger
I won't be hurt-any longer
Cause I feel sure-I won't pace the floor
No more dear-when you walk out the door

TIME IS MY ENEMY

Honey I sit here wondering
Did I do something wrong
Was I really wrong in thinking
It's to you that I belong

Time is my enemy
I just can't understand
Why I fell for you so quickly
And why I want you for my man

My days are long and empty
My nights lonely and blue
I spend my time wondering
Why I haven't heard from you

I daydream oh so constantly
Of moments that we've shared
I have nightmares of you mocking me
Asking, 'Did you think I really cared?"

I can't go on not knowing
If I were a fool for you
Was I just a play-thing
Simply for you to use

MEMORIES

Memories are all that I have left
Of the love for me you once possessed
Memories are all that I think of
But they no longer give me happiness

For when I think back on all we use to share
And think about now and you being bored
I'm beginning to think you really don't care
And what you want is your freedom more and more

Well darling go on your merry way
I won't be blamed for another day
About you being bored-missing out on things
The good times you want and other sweet flings

Painful memories are all I possess
While you chase for your happiness
Painful memories-of times once shared
Of good times and bad—when you once cared

TIME SHARED WITH ME

I am in love—but my love—is no longer my own
He's found another to make and share his home
I am alone—but he stays on my mind
I find me looking forward to having any of his time
    Spent with me-shared with me time spent just looking
    Or talking—or loving but at least spent with me
When we're on the phone and I hear his silky voice
Does he realize that I'm suppose to be his choice
Why-when he speaks—does his voice affect me so
Cold chills run through me-from my head down to my toes
    Looking forward to time shared with me time spent just
    Hugging, rubbing or loving-but at least spent with me
        I know that soon the day will come
        We'll be together again as one
        Kissing and loving all the time
        Cause he will finally be all mine
Now days are slow and my nights long and blue
Looking forward to that day when their thing is through
And I'll have my mate to myself day and night
Filling his life with sheer delight
    And he'll look forward to time shared with me
    Time spent just living talking and giving
    But at least shared with me

GOOD LUCK

You know you bring me good luck
Whenever I hear your voice
And feel your gentle touch
And know that I'm your choice

You know you bring me good luck
When I look into your eyes
And know that there is no such
Thing I can't realize

in knowing you
And holding you tight
And loving you hard
With all my might
In having you
And your kisses so sweet
And needing you
Whenever we meet

Cause you know you bring me good luck
Such a bright glow
When I touch you
And hold you close

You know you bring me good luck
When I lay down my head
And when I feel I'm love struck
When we kiss on the bed

I know you
I love holding you tight
Love loving you hard
With all my might
Love having you
And your kisses so sweet
Love needing you
Whenever we meet

I WAS GOOD

I was good for bad times-and pleasure too
I was good for everything-when I dealt with you
But you let me know-you didn't mind if I'd go
On about my way-and suffer-lost of love today

I was good for-sweet times-and tenderness
You must admit-that I gave you-marital bliss
But you-let me know you didn't mind if I'd go
On about my way-and suffer-lost of love today

You didn't want me-not the way-I thought you would
You didn't keep me-like-I thought you should
And as I walked away-to face another lonely day
I realize I was lonely-with you-any old way

But I was good for-your bad times-and good ones too
I was good for everything we thought we should do
But I'll go on my way-and won't regret the day
When you'll have to pay-instead of play

For I was good for bad times-and pleasure too
I was good for everything-when I dealt with you
But you let me know-you didn't mind if I'd go
On my way-and have you suffer-lost of love today

A SONG IN MY HEART

I miss you-you put a song in my heart
I miss you-every since we've been apart
I miss you-I I count the hours as they pass
And I wonder should I miss you
    Just how long will this feeling last

I want you-with every breath I take
I want you-so much I'm beginning to ache
I want you-but my darling you can't see
You can't see how I'm feeling
    For I don't have you here with me

I must go on-with these feelings I possess
For we don't know-if we can have true happiness
If you feel the way I do-would you want to take a chance
For us to share our time my love-in a one on one romance
    For I feel that

I love you-but I'm just afraid to trust
Feelings between us-but love somehow I must
I feel I love you-and yes I know you care
Before I grow to love you long and hard I must forget the fear

    Of being hurt by love again-so soon hon
    But I miss you and I want a one on one
    We've shared some time and you appear to be sincere
    And if that's your indication
        Then love I need you here

For I miss you-you put a song in my heart
I miss you-every since we've been apart
I miss you-I count the hours as they pass
And I wonder should I miss you
    Just how long this feeling will last

PLUS FIVE SENSES

I have seen the highest peaks of the mountains
I have seen the deepest depths of the sea
I have been around the world
Since I've been your only girl
You have brought out the best within me

I have felt the tender softness of the rain
I have felt the silky warmness of the wind
I have felt the suns' bright rays
I have felt the moon beams play
You have brought out the best that's within

I have smelled the aroma of an orchid
I have smelled the sweet breath of fresh snow
I have smelled a blade of grass
And have sensed an angel pass
You have brought out the best this I know

I have heard the soft whisper in a seashell
I have heard the gentle footsteps of a friend
I have heard the highest note
I have heard a small leaf float
You have brought out the best felt within

I have tasted the honey of your body
I have tasted the saltiness of your tears
I have tasted the love you give
I have tasted the life you live
You have brought out the best without fears

SOME FOLKS

Some folks tried to tell me-that there was no such thing as love
Some folks tried to tell me-but I said it's you that I think of
Some folks tried to tell me-I'd be sitting feeling blue
They tried to tell me all of that-but I continued seeing you

Some folks tried to tell me-you would make me feel this way
You would make me wish for love and wait on you everyday
Somehow I wouldn't listen-I shut them out of my mind
I wouldn't listen when they told me-that I was wasting time

But honey they don't know the reason why I feel within
Is because you love me also cause I was heading where you've been
I was searching for a lover-I was searching for a friend
But when I met you-I found both-to last until the end

Now some folks try to tell you-the same old song about me
Some folks try to tell you-our-relationship should not be
Some folks try to tell you-that I ain't just no good
But did they also tell you-they would take me if they could

Some folks will not let us be—for they are envious inside
Some folks want to see us fail-but those are feelings that they hide
But all those folks we should let go-leave them in their misery
Don't allow them to mind our business-and make them all leave us be

That way-no folks will try to tell us-anything that's wrong
No folks will have to wish us well-no folks will hang along
Filling our hearts with negatives-on what we choose to do
So the bottom line to you my dear-is-no folks can come between us two

BESIDE ME

I want a lady of my very own-someone to share a loving-happy home
She don't have to be a beauty queen-but she must with me be a team
Walking beside me all aglow-walking beside me-inward she'll know

    I want her near me, all day and all night long
    I want her near me, when I feel I'm not strong
    She's not a mat to dry wet aching feet
    Nor does she has to be a quick hot seat
    Walking beneath me or behind me
    I want my lady to really see

        I've dreamed of loving such a pearl like her
        I never thought that dream would ever occur
        But now that we've found each other
        We will work at being together
        And I won't let her slip away
        As we share each and every day

I found my lady-she's my very own
And I will keep her-she is to whom I belong
To love and God knows really keep
To hold and squeeze when I lay down to sleep

    She walks beside me-that's where she'll always be
    She has a special place-deep-down-inside of me
    To treasure—and last forever
    With pleasure-and we'll stay together

        I found my lady-she walks beside me
        I found my lady-she's deep inside me
        I found my lady

SONGS

I look out of the window
    With my head against the screen
I breakup within silently
    I stifle back my scream
I waited for you patiently
    And waited oh so long
And while I sat here waiting dear
    I decided to write songs
Songs of pain and loneliness
    Songs of missing you
Songs of wanting you so much
    Hoping you feel the same way too
Do you want me for your own
    And as more than just a friend
Or are you trying to tell me dear
    That you want it to end
I lie across my bed and write
    And how I wish so much
That you were lying next to me
    And thrilling me with your touch

WHAT IS THIS HOLD

What is this hold my love
    That you have on me
Why is it obvious my dear
    I feel such misery
When I don't see you
    To have, hold and touch
It really leaves me aching
    O h so very much

Why do I feel empty
    Why do I feel pain
Is it because-I'm afraid
    I won't see you again
I ache to hold you
    And keep you near
I long to have you
    For keeps my dear

I am so damn lonely
    Lonely and blue
I sit here just waiting
    With nothing to do
What is this hold my love
    That you have on me
Also tell me why
    I feel so much misery

WHEN I'M AT HOME

I want someone   just to walk with me
Someone somewhere   who won't let me be
All alone sitting   by the phone
Sitting alone   in an unhappy home

I want someone   walking by my side
I don't need someone   on whom I can't rely
When I need love   when I want a kiss
Don't need someone   whom I know I'll miss

           When I am at home
             Watching TV
                Sitting alone
                    Oh in misery
           When I'm at home
             And there's only me
                Feeling in pain
                    That's not suppose to be

Why oh why   it's all because
I want someone   to walk by my side
Someone   somewhere

BE FOR REAL

I love you. There's no greater feeling
Then the feeling I possess   For they are ones of true happiness
"Be for real.' I tell myself, I constantly remind me
For I am all alone and don't have to be

Cause you're not sure you want me
I am from your past
And the feelings you once possess
We don't know if they will last

I need you   I love you   I want you by my side
I need you as my lover and to be my guide
I need you to help me make this house a home
I need you also to stop being on the roam

I need you to share my life
This is a figure of speech I know
The one of me wanting to be a wife
To a lover on the go

But honey I need you to make my life
The dream I've dreamed of
Of wanting love, but still I know
I'm not allowed to love

I can not give   I cannot live
I'm not allowed to be myself
Let me hold squeeze and need you
Stop putting me on a shelf

Darling let me love you and have you for my own
Let me love you sweet heart   let us build a happy home
I'm only singing what I feel   it hurts because it's real
I'll be happy with just you   I admit it's really true

Sweetheart I really need you
And I want you by my side
Honey I want you
So on each other   let's rely

PRESCRIPTION -3RD ATTEMPT

Another day has gone by, and I sit and wonder why
I didn't see your smiling face, nor did I feel your warm embrace
Are you ok? Are you aright? Did you have a silly fight?
Make the choice-come to my door; come be with me forever more
For I'll love you-never make you blue;
I'll make you happy with all I say and do

> Darling I need you here with me
> God why won't you let it be
> Let us be a prescription for love between us two

Evening is coming and I'm all alone
and he hasn't called me-I sit by the phone
but I'll wait patiently for I know he will be
here by my side reaching for me
Darkness surrounds us-we're holding tight
We will enfold each other tonight
But when the daybreak streaks the sky
you will get up and I'll wonder why

> another day will be going by
> and I'll be wiping my tear stained eyes
> hoping and praying the day will come
> when we'll be together-completely as one

4ᵀᴴ PRESCRIPTION

You took your time to walk into my life
At the moment I was suffering from stress and strife
You took me in your arms and asked me what I thought of
As you being my prescription for love

You tilted my head up with your hand beneath my chin
You made warmness grow sweetly from deep within
You held me tenderly; asked me to try and see
That our special love was meant to be

        I was lonely   feeling blue
        Feeling depressed with nothing to do
        Always crying   feeling pain
        Until the day   you finally came

You promised me you'd always be by my side
You promised me you'd always be my guide
You asked me just what I thought of
As you darling, being my prescription for love

SONGS:

Rap

MOMS' RAP

I'm going to rap to you my child-since you listen to rap
Have a seat for a while-and listen to this chat
I want to save you from this bull-which you're caught up in
Tell you where you're going, been-and just where you'll end
      I want to talk about your friends—and you personally
      I want to talk about your kin-and how you choose to be
      I'm going to tell you about everything-good and bad
      And the choice you have to make to be glad or sad
My child, you know, I know, you know that you are smart
And I've always known you've known from the very start
However you're using your brain—in a negative way
Trying to be slick and get over-from day to day
      You're thinking that you are-but really you're not
      And it you keep thinking that-your brain will only rot
      You should be using your intelligence-to achieve in life
      For yourself, your children and soon maybe a wife
I've noticed how well mannered—you are with others
Yet you and your friends are disrespecting mothers
You think we owe you something-and it's very apparent
That you resent us very much for being-a single parent
      We-go to work-each and every day
      And you think that's the time-for you to have your way
      You hooky from school-your friends drop by
      You drink my booze and y'all smoke and get high
You put on the rap and turn it very loud
Busting the block with sounds that are foul
You use my bed and hide the sheets
I can tell what's going on when I hear the feet
      Of your friends rushing quickly out the door
      I know they've robbed me blind again once more
      And by you feeling lonely, scared and down
      You'll let them in again when I'm not around
You're extremely handsome—that's for sure
But looks won't get you anywhere in this world
Six feet three with a beautiful tan
Running around with an out stretched hand

"Give me twenty, loan me fifty-I just can't wait
To take that lovely chick out on a date."
There's a different one for morning-noon-and night
And some of the girls really look a sight
Some are tall-some short-some fat-some skinny
Some look as though they slept with every and any
Some are loud and wrong-some are quiet and shy
But not nary one could look me in the eye
Your boys are with you—comparing notes
The girls don't even know that your boys are casting votes
About what they did-and who was the best
Exchanging names and all the rest
And if you got the piece belonging to your boy
Then he'd rush you when he saw you cause you had his toy
Then what do you do, lay low for a while
Then when you go out, get chased for a mile
While out in the streets you get high with the rest
And then they kick your butt to show you who is best
Keep it up my son and you'll be on the run
With life passing you by-do you think that's fun?
You will end up like some men-who act no good
Not able to take care of home like they know they should
Running back and forth between lovers and wife
Not knowing who or what they wanted out of life
Like one with no where to lay his head
And losing everything he had instead
Walking down the street with giant size holes
In his dirty shirt and paper thin soles
Resenting everyone who looked his way
He pulls out his pipe and smokes some jay
Another cons family out of their money
And then becomes mad cause he can't be their honey
Wise up my child and go back to school
Live by the norm instead of the rule
If you don't do that—then find a job
Don't end up on the streets being part of a mob
Cussing-beating-and robbing your very own
Or sticking your hand out for a loan

Other races of people are helping each other
They don't let kids rob and beat their mother
 Most things you do out of loneliness
 Because you feel no one gives a piss
 Well, I do my son-I love you very much
 But I'll no longer tolerate such and such
Either change for the better or leave my home
Learn to do for yourself if you choose to roam
If you make a bad choice and land in jail
I don't have the scratch to pay your bail
 But here's the real deal which is on my mind
 You won't be living with me all the time
 But while you're here you're to clean your room
 If you know what's good for you-you'll do it soon
Cause your so called good thing has come to an end
You may find yourself living with a so called friend
And your so called friends—thinking this is a hotel
Come back again—so I can really yell

Dedicated to peer-pressured young adults of single parents

I AM NOW AWARE

I am aware of you doing me wrong
I am aware that it won't be long
Before one of us suggest we go separate ways
Be alone-it's possible-not a poem or song

I am aware that I'm sharing you
I'm aware also of other things you do
I'm aware it doesn't mean a damn thing to you
If we look at it from you point of view

I am aware that we were never meant to be
I'm aware that what you had for me was fantasy
You feel I was your biggest mistake, you see
Cause I stopped you from treating me as you pleased

I compare myself with Betty, Sarah, Tyra and Bess
And even compared myself with all the rest
I'm beginning to think you have realized—oh yes
Out of all of your choices-that I was your best

Sarah and Bess still have a hold on you
And they both have held it since 2002
Betty got hers in 04 with you
And Tyra and all your latest ones are still too new

You've never made me feel you were mine alone
It's been over seven years since I've had a happy home
And they are the reasons why I was left alone
There was very strong evidence you were on the roam

I'm aware now you have no desire
And there is nothing I would do to even inspire
You to have faith in me and try
To set me aglow set me afire

We have several problems, you say you care
But it's the blame that you won't share
I'm not perfect and neither are you my dear
So try for once in life to be fair

I still love you and want you but I won't compete
Because in the end I will be beat
By your desire for others and being indiscreet
Your freedom's there for I don't need the heat
All I ask is that you not think of me
In a negative way cause I set you free
I want to break up, want you to let me be
I want to lock up my heart and destroy the key

There's one other thing deep within my heart
And I just want to say it before we part
I was always loyal, loved and wanted you desperately
But now honey, goodbye, I want to make a new start

MODEL STAR

For the evidence… you were heaven sent…I know you were, baby…And from the love of you…all the things you do…you're my posing star, baby Come and take my hand…and walk with me…down the runway…of ecstasy…and I love the way…you shine on the scene…girl you need to be in my magazine…cause you're an angel, baby…a Model Star to me…You're an angel girl…a Model Star for me

To the Lord I cried, send a lady…and into my life you came…Oh the power of prayer, He sent an angel…and nothing has been the same come and take my hand…with me understand…I am your man, I'll do the best I can…down that runway run.. straight into my arms…baby, I'll protect you from any and all harm…cause you're an angel baby…A Model Star to me …you're an angel girl …A Model Star to me

(FEMALE RAP) Yes honey, I was heaven sent- do whatever you can to keep me in your life. I'll be your angel and I'm hell bent to be your friend, your lover and maybe your wife…as you hold me in your arms take time to cultivate the feelings you possess…you may protect me from harm and let the time we share be filled with total happiness…The butterflies won't let me be, now as I think of you…my stomach flutters constantly…I don't know what to do…my arms ache to hold you tight, I don't know what to do…my arms ache to hold you tight and never let you go…my heart ache to say the words of how I love you so…Honey I want, desire and truly need this opportunity…to make the most of this relationship so we can live happily. So, for the evidence. I was heaven sent to be the lady in your life. I am the posing star, I am the lady, may have, one day, as your wife. You're my lady…you were heaven sent…you're my loving angel, baby…these feelings I possess…are joy and happiness for you're my Posing star…baby…be my model dear…be my starlight here…on this runway of ecstasy. And I love the way you shine on the scene…girl I am putting you in my magazine. Cause you're an angel lady…A Model Star to me…you're an angel girl, a Model Star to me.

IN MEMORY OF MY AGENT

Hi Ames, Hey, I hope you're doing okay
I have some bad news to share with you today
My agent, lawyer and I were in a car accident
We had just got out of a meeting and this is how it went
We had pulled into traffic, and while waiting for the light
My agent looked up and felt something wasn't right
She looked up and said, Soul that car is going to run into us"
She said "duck down" but I could not move ---the car hit us in a rush
When the old lady smashed into us I went over the top
I landed on top of my agent 'O God why wasn't it stopped?"
Her head smashed into the window, causing glass to go into her brain
 My left leg was smashed beyond repair, "O God this is insane."
My lawyer was in the back seat with something stuck in his chest
I have more to tell you so listen to the rest
Ames, I am sad to say, "O God I have lost my leg."
"My God, I am sure if I could have foreseen, I'm sure I would have
begged---you to save my agent for I feel I am to blame
Because I landed on top of her, though it wasn't my aim
She lost her life, I feel I killed her- Jesus help me please
Take away the guilt, the suffering, put my mind at ease.
Don't you hear what I am saying, this is hard on me
Cause she is dead, dead, dead and I feel she should not be
I love you my friend, pray for us, help me to understand
Why she slipped away from me before I could hold her hand
I could not attend the services when they laid her to rest
I couldn't say good-bye so I became weak, O God is this a test
 She made me who I am in this industry
And I really made it bid because she believed in me
My agent deserves a tribute to keep her memory alive
For she was with me 24/7 not just 9 to 5
I really want to do something so she won't be forgotten
I also want to loose the guilt for it makes me feel rotten
Thank God I have my daughter who is by my side

We share our tears together for I have no pride
I know friends and associates wondered what became of me
They did not hear from me when I lost my leg below my knee
For a month and a half I had kept to myself
While I kept my agent's memories way up upon a shelf
"Lord Jesus, I ask of you what am I to do next
I feel guilt and pain and burdened. I feel so perplexed."
Lord Jesus guide my footsteps as I learn to walk again
Help me memorize my agent for that is my aim
I have fame and fortune all because of her
Because she believed in me- that we can concur
Let me feel Lord Jesus-you beside my side
Let me feel you always as my GOD and guide
You say you are the way, the truth and the life
Help me Father, please help me to get right without strife.

PRAYERS TO GOD

THE SAME LORD OVER ALL IS *RICH* UNTO *ALL* THAT CALL UPON HIM.

Romans 10:12

EVENING, MORNING AND AT NOON, WILL I PRAY AND CRY ALOUD; AND HE SHALL HEAR MY VOICE.

Ps 55:17

THE LORD'S PRAYER

Our Father which art in heaven, Hallowed be thy name,
Thy kingdom come, Thy will be done on earth, as it is
in heaven. Give us this day our daily bread, And forgive
us our debts, as we for give our debtors. And lead us not
into temptation, but deliver us from evil: For thine is the
kingdom, and the power, and the glory, forever. (Amen).

THE LORD'S PR AYER

Our Father who art in heaven, Hallowed be thy name,
Thy kingdom come, Thy will be done on earth, as it is
in heaven. Give us this day our daily bread, And forgive
us our trespasses, as we for those those who trespass
against us. And lead us not into temptation, but deliver
us from evil: For thine is the kingdom, and the power,
and the glory, forever. (Amen).

St. Matthew 6:9-13

A PSALM OF PR AISE-PSALM 100:1-5

Make a joyful noise unto the Lord, all ye lands. Serve the Lord with
gladness: come before his presence with singing.

Know ye that the Lord he is God: it is he that hath made us, as not we
ourselves; we are his people, and the sheep of his pasture.

Enter into his gates with thanksgiving, and into his courts with praise:
be thankful unto him and bless his name.

For the Lord is good; his mercy is everlasting; and his truth endureth
to all generations.

A PSALM OF DAVID-PSALM 23:1-6

The Lord is my shepherd; I shall not want;

He maketh me to lie down in green pastures: he leadeth me beside
the still waters.

He restoreth my soul: he leadeth me in the paths of righteousness
for his name's sake.

Yea, though I walk through the valley of the shadow of death, I will
fear no evil: for thou art with me; thy rod and thy staff they comfort me.

Thou preparest a table before me in the presence of my enemies:
thou anointest my head with oil; my cup runneth over.

Surely goodness and mercy shall follow me all the days of my life:
and I will dwell in the house of the Lord for ever.

MY PERSONAL PRAYER

Thank you Lord God Almighty for allowing me to open my eyes
to see a brand new day.

Please forgive me for my thoughts and sins. Please forgive my mom,
son, sisters, brothers, relatives and friends for their thoughts and sins.

Please walk with us Lord: in life and in death, in lightness and in
darkness, awake and asleep protecting us from all evil, all harm
and all danger.

Please Lord allow my relatives and friends to find employment, have
job security and stay gainfully employed. Please bless us with good
health and prosperity, dear Lord and please keep us all from being
incarcerated.

Please help all creation to stop lying, cheating and stealing and please help
us all to stop smoking, drinking and doing drugs.

Please give us a clean heart and spirit, dear Lord, and give us a spirit of discernment.

These and other blessings I ask of you in the name of
Lord Jesus Christ of Nazareth, in the name of Lord God Almighty
Jehovah and in the name of Allah.

(Amen).

GOD

"He gave us his breath and we became a living soul."
God created man in his image and likeness and in doing so;
man has body, soul and spirit dependent on God. He created
woman as man's helper. He included in his creation our head
and body.

He gave us two eyes to see-one nose to smell-a tongue to taste-
two ears to hear-lips to bless—a mind to perceive-two arms to hold-
a heart to feel-two legs to entwine-two feet to move us about
a heart to feel-a body to house his spirit-and we do not use any of
the members the way God intended.

Our hearts, the greatest part of all, we fail to use to love and live.
Our mind-to choose life, good and right; over death, evil and wrong.
Our ears believe half of what we hear because we fail to listen.
Our eyes-blind by the smote within, so we fail to see fully.
Our tongue speaks words of love and in the same breath curse with hatred.
Our arms strike out instead of enfolding. Our legs run away instead of
standing and beholding the beauty of life and love. Our bodies are
being used; no morals-no values, to express inordinate affections of lust,
instead of as a temple to house his spirit. Our feet run to and from evil.
Our hands are murdering helpless babies. Our breath is being corrupted
by drugs, alcohol and cigarettes.

It is ironic Jesus was wounded on his head by wearing a crown of thorns,
his mouth—by drinking vinegar, and being pierced in his hands, feet and side.
Those are the same members of our bodies which cause us to sin greatly.
So I pray to God, "Please hear me. Grant me the will to live in this world in
the flesh and in your world in the spirit."

"ABBA FATHER"

In 1988—I learned to pray by saying 'Abba Father' when I need him and also by praying 'The Lord's Prayer.'

God spoke to me one night in a dream. He said, "if you *ever need me* just call *Abba Father*.

I searched my bible until I found the words 'Abba Father'. I found it three times; Galatians 4:6, Romans 8:15 and St. Mark14:36.

There is no doubt; I am his child for I never knew such a word existed. He watches over me, protects me, and provide for me. He's always there. I love him. I praise him, I give thanks to him and I honor him. Bless God.

MORNING PRAYER FOR GUIDANCE

Jesus, today is a day I've never experienced before. Please hear my prayer Make your presence in my heart be known by me today in some small way.
Please guide my life and watch over me. Also, love and lead my loved ones far and near.

In whatever we set out to do, let us do so remembering that you are guiding us so that we will be pleasing in your sight. Turn us away from our iniquities and let your Spirit of Righteousness dwell in us today.

Thank you for hearing my prayer. Thank you for granting the desires of my heart. Thank you for all the blessings you have bestowed us seen and unseen. (Amen)

NOON PRAYER FOR PROSPERITY

Lord God, In the name of Jesus, I come before you again. In Joshua 1:5-9 you stated you will be with me, you will not forsake me, you will not fail me. You told me to be strong, very courageous, be not afraid or dismayed. You told me to meditate in your word so that I may observe and do all that is written in it; by doing so you would make my way prosperous and I shall have good success.

Hear me Lord God, my heavenly Father. I need your help and your wisdom for me to succeed. Bless me with the same. Bless me and my loved ones with prosperity. Oh Lord as in Nehemiah 1:11, I beseech thee, let now thine ear be attentive to the prayer of thy servant, and to the prayers of the servants who desire to fear thy name: and prosper, I thy servant, pray thee this day, and grant us mercy in the sight of men.

Thank you for hearing my prayer. Thank you for all the blessings you are bestowing on me, in Jesus name. (Amen)

PRAYER TO GIVE THANKS

Father God, in the name of Jesus I come before you. Please hear my voice. I come before you today to say thank you. Thank you God, for everything. I've read where Jesus healed lepers and only one came back to thank him. It is written, in everything give thanks. Father God, if I remember to do so, I will, for I find the only time I say thank you is when something good happens and I respond instantly by saying "Thank God" or "Thank you Jesus."

Right now I want to thank you for all of your blessings which you are bestowing upon me daily. Since they are so numerous, I will say thank you for everything. I will also thank you especially for your love, grace, mercy, justice, and compassion while granting the desires of my heart. Thank you for choosing me to follow you.

Thank you for my food, clothing, shelter, labor, friends, associates and loved ones. Thank you even more so for opening my eyes and ears, for giving me a clean heart and for forgiving me my sins. Thank you for allowing me to learn of and trying to understand your laws, statues, precepts and judgments.

Thank you for restoring to me the spirits of peace, joy, contentment, faith, hope, endurance and patience. Thank you for allowing me to seek truth and righteousness. Thank you for humbling me. Thank you for teaching me how to live, how to love, how to pray, how to watch, how to seek, how to knock and how to ask. Thank you God for everything. (Amen)

PRAYER SEEKING FORGIVENESS

ABBA FATHER, please hear my prayer. I humbly come before you, in the name of Jesus seeking forgiveness for my sins. Father, I was wrong in what I did, and I am truly sorry. Please forgive me. Please blot out the sins I've committed. My heart is so heavy burdened. My conscious is really bothering me. Lord God, I feel such deep remorse.

Not only have I sinned against you, but I have hurt others emotionally. Please forgive me. Father please give me a clean heart. Please remove all fear from me, and then I would have no excuse to turn to alcohol. Please give me a strong will power to help me in my fight against being a servant to sin. Please give me the determination not to willfully sin.

Lord I need prayer right now. I really need others to pray for me on my behalf. I can't find the right words to say, but you do know my heart. Please help me father.

My eyes did not truly open until I read the words, you gave us the gift of life and what we do with it is our gift to you. I'm asking you to help me, show me the way, let your will be done.

Thank you for listening to me. I feel better already. Thank you for answering
my prayer. (Amen)

Phyllis Ames-Bey

This will Certify that

Phyllis B. Ames Bey

is a member in good standing

International Society of Poets

and has attained the Distinction

Member

with all the privileges accorded thereto
and is recognized for support of
the Society's principles of
Peace – Education – Accomplishment
Charity – Equality

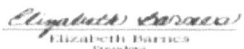

Elizabeth Barnes
President

The National Authors Registry

In recognition of literary excellence for

My Song Of Solomon To You

the directors of the National Authors Registry hereby confer upon

Phyllis Ames

This

President's Award
for Literary Excellence 2001

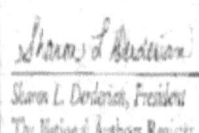

Sharon L. Derderian, President
The National Authors Registry

Iliad 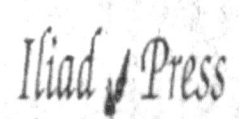 Press

The National Authors Registry

In recognition of literary excellence for

My Song of Solomon To You

the independent judges of the
Fall 1999 Iliad Literary Awards Program
Hereby confer upon

Phyllis Ames

This certificate of

Honorable Mention

Sharon L. Denbaum, Executive Editor

My Song Of Solomon To You
by Phyllis Ames

"Set me as a seal upon your heart"
   This would ensure we'd never part.
"Set me as a seal upon your arms"
   To protect our love from any harm.
"For love my dear is as strong as death"
   But when life has ended, the love is left
"And jealousy is as strong as the grave"
   And envy is all our associates gave.
"The coals thereof are coals of fire"
   Love is what jealous people desire.
"And they do have a vehement flame"
   But so does our love, for that's our aim
"Many waters cannot quench love"
   It's an everlasting flame from God above
"Neither can the floods drown it"
   So ours will be forever lit.
If you would give me all of your love,
   We can defeat all they think of.
Daryl, let me share my life with you,
   Let us share everything we do.
Help me keep our love alive,
   For it is strong and our survive.
So, set me as a seal upon your heart,
   This will ensure we'd never part.

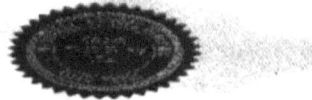

"1999"
Honorable
Mention

Sharon L. Davidson

Iliad 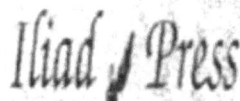 Press

The National Authors Registry

In recognition of literary excellence for

Weather Masterpiece

the independent judges of the
Fall 1999 Iliad Literary Awards Program
hereby confer upon

Phyllis Ames

This certificate of

Honorable Mention

Sharon L. Anderson

Sharon L. Anderson, Executive Editor

Weather Masterpiece

by Phyllis Ames

I am the mist, at the break of dawn,
  Lingering with you, all the day long.
I am the breeze on a hot summer day,
  Caressing and cooling you in every way.
I am the moon, lighting your path at night,
  The star keeping you company, shining bright.
The sun beaming brilliantly during the day,
  From dawn to dusk, with you I'll stay.
I am the heavy fog which clouds your mind,
  By causing misunderstanding some of the time.
I am the storm cloud, when things go wrong,
  But calmness will come when I am calm.
I am the ray of sunlight in the midst of the storm,
  Look within my heart for light and warmth.
I am the rainbow, but beware of my illusion.
  You may experience euphoria or even confusion.
I am the heat in the summer, cold in the winter,
  You feel the same in your heart, now that I've entered.
I am the softness of spring, dryness of autumn,
  Your heart feels the same, when it caught in.
I am the rain which causes the flowers to grow,
  I am the aroma of the same when my breezes blow.
I am the honey to be gathered not only by the bees,
  I am the nectar to be savored by you with care.
But don't allow me to be the essence in your life,
  Because your happiness may depend on my peace or strife.
And I wouldn't want you to suffer pain or delay,
  While being your weather masterpiece, for you deserve today.

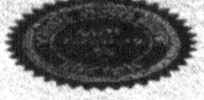

June 3, 2008

Phyllis Ames_bey

Dear Phyllis

I am delighted to inform you that your poem "My Masterpiece" has been awarded our prestigious Editor's Choice Award because it displays a unique perspective and original creativity — judged to be the qualities most found in exceptional poetry. Congratulations on your achievement.

Your poem is also featured in a Deluxe Hardbound Edition, which, as expected, will soon be sold out. We have, however, reserved a limited number of copies that are now available only to poets included in this distinctive volume. Because you are one of these poets, and if you haven't already ordered a copy, or wish to reserve additional copies, this is your last opportunity to do so.

Oh, and one final note. Many people have asked if we can make available a commemorative plaque to present their poetry in formal fashion. We are glad to be able to do this. Your poem can be beautifully typeset on archive quality vellum with your choice of borders, then mounted on a walnut-finish plaque under lucite. The 10-1/2 by 13 inch plaques are truly impressive ways to exhibit your work. They also make wonderful gifts. Please use the enclosed material for further information. Again, congratulations on your achievement.

Editor's Choice Award

Presented to

Phyllis Ames_bey

June 2008

For Outstanding Achievement in Poetry

Presented by

poetry.com and the International Library of Poetry

poetry.COM

Howard Ely
Managing Editor

The National Authors Registry

This is to Certify that

Phyllis Ames

Has met the standards of publication, and is eligible for membership in

The National Authors Registry

having been sponsored by

Iliad Press

an imprint of Cader Publishing, Ltd.

And is inducted on **February 16, 2001** and shall hereafter be entitled to append the initials R.A. (Registered Author) after her name.

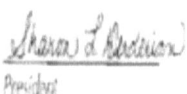

President

The National Authors Registry

This is to Certify that

Phyllis Ames

Has met the standards of publication, and is eligible for membership in

The National Authors Registry

having been sponsored by

Iliad Press

an imprint of Cader Publishing, Ltd.

And is inducted on **December 30, 1999** and shall hereafter be entitled to append the initials R.A. (Registered Author) after her name.

President

April 8, 2008

VIP #A677947 – AHV 3 L
Phyllis Ames Bey

Dear Phyllis,

I am delighted to inform you that your poem "My Song of Solomon to You" has been awarded our prestigious Editor's Choice Award because it displays a unique perspective and original creativity judged to be the qualities most found in exceptional poetry. Congratulations on your achievement.

Your poem is also featured in a Deluxe Hardbound Edition, which, as expected, will soon be sold out. We have, however, reserved a limited number of copies that are now available only to poets included in this distinctive volume. Because you are one of these poets, and if you haven't already ordered a copy, or wish to obtain additional copies, this is your last opportunity to do so.

Oh, and one final note. Many people have asked if we can make available a commemorative plaque to present their poetry in formal fashion. We are glad to be able to do this. Your poem can be beautifully typeset on archive quality vellum with your choice of borders, then mounted on a walnut finish plaque under lucite. The 10 1/2 by 13 inch plaques are truly impressive ways to exhibit your work. They also make wonderful gifts. Please see the enclosed material for further information. Again, congratulations on your achievement.

Editor's Choice Award

Presented to

Phyllis Ames Bey

April 2008

For Outstanding Achievement in Poetry

Presented by

poetry.com and the International Library of Poetry

poetry.COM

Harvard Bey
Managing Editor

March 8, 2005

VIP 66730926 - 333 3
Phyllis Ames

Dear Phyllis,

I am delighted to inform you that your poem "My Song of Solomon to You" has been awarded our prestigious Editor's Choice Award because it displays a unique perspective and original creativity – judged to be the qualities most found in exceptional poetry. Congratulations on your achievement.

Your poem is also featured in a Deluxe Hardbound Edition, which, as expected, will soon be sold out. We have, however, reserved a limited number of copies that are now available only to poets included in this distinctive volume. Because you are one of these poets, and if you haven't already ordered a copy, or wish to obtain additional copies, this is your last opportunity to do so.

Oh, and one final note. Many people have asked if we can make available a commemorative plaque to present their poetry in formal fashion. We are glad to be able to do this. Your poem can be beautifully typeset on archive quality vellum with your choice of borders, then mounted on a walnut-finish plaque under lucite. The 10 1/2 by 13 inch plaques are truly impressive ways to exhibit your work. They also make wonderful gifts. Please see the enclosed material for further information. Again, congratulations on your achievement.

Editor's Choice Award

Presented to

Phyllis Ames
March 2005

For Outstanding Achievement in Poetry
Presented by
poetry.com and the International Library of Poetry

poetry.COM

Howard Ely
Managing Editor

www.ingramcontent.com/pod-product-compliance
Lightning Source LLC
Chambersburg PA
CBHW021608120626
46545CB00001B/132